Betty Saw's
Everyday Cooking
Essential Asian Home-Style Recipes

Betty Saw

Marshall Cavendish Cuisine

The publisher wishes to thank Mr Keng of Tong Meng Sern Antiques Arts & Crafts and Charlie Lim for the loan of their valuable antiques and tableware; Mdm Fauseah A. Bakar and Mdm Hamidah Omar for the use of their lovely tablecloths.

Food Preparation: Gourmet Haven, except for the dishes on pages 11, 13, 75, 131, 139, 151 and 165 by Mdm Cheong Mee Siew

Photographer: Charlie Lim

Other Marshall Cavendish Offices:
Marshall Cavendish Corporation, 800 Westchester Ave, Suite N-641, Rye Brook, NY 10573, USA • Marshall Cavendish International (Thailand) Co Ltd, 253 Asoke, 16th Floor, Sukhumvit 21 Road, Klongtoey Nua, Wattana, Bangkok 10110, Thailand • Marshall Cavendish (Malaysia) Sdn Bhd, Times Subang, Lot 46, Subang Hi-Tech Industrial Park, Batu Tiga, 40000 Shah Alam, Selangor Darul Ehsan, Malaysia

Marshall Cavendish is a trademark of Times Publishing Limited

Printed in Singapore

Preface

It has always been one of my greatest interests to collect and write down the recipes popularly prepared and enjoyed in home kitchens in the 1970s and 1980s. It has not been an easy task, however, as most people did not write down their recipes. Recipes were casually shared among the womenfolk as they gathered together in the evening after a hard day's work and chatted or gossiped about the day's events. Recipes were also closely-guarded within families and handed down from generation to generation with the matriarch personally taking a daughter, daughter-in-law or granddaughter under her wing, and teaching her as they went about their daily chores.

Another difficulty in sourcing out these recipes is the fact that there was no proper means of measurement then. People simply used a handful of this and a pinch of that, and cooked according to taste and experience. With changing mindsets and the greater inclination to eat out nowadays, these recipes have also gradually been forgotten, and not many people know how to prepare and cook these dishes anymore.

It has been an uphill task tracking down these recipes, but to keep them from being lost and forgotten, I have worked to compile these 75 recipes in this book. The cooking methods have been carefully changed and adapted to make the recipes suitable for use in the modern kitchen. I have also put in measurements and tested them to ensure that they are correct and that the taste and dish remained authentic.

This collection of recipes will bring back fond memories for some of us. For others, I hope this book will serve as a showcase of Asian dishes to share with family and friends the good old fashioned way.

Betty Saw

Contents

Vegetables

Snacks & Desserts

Glossary

Basic Recipes

Weights & Measures

POULTRY

Salt Baked Chicken

Preparation time: 20 minutes   Cooking time: 1 hour   Serves 8

Ingredients

Whole chicken	1, about 1.5 kg
Dark soy sauce	1 tsp
Spring onions (scallions)	2, coarsely chopped
Chinese angelica root (*tong kwai*)	3 slices or 2 whole star anise
Coarse salt	5 kg
Mulberry or greaseproof paper	3 sheets, 70-cm square

Seasoning

Salt	1 tsp
Ginger juice	2 tsp
Brandy, Chinese rice or rose wine	1 Tbsp

Ginger and Spring Onion Dip

Shallot oil	4 Tbsp (page 175)
Salt	1 tsp
Ginger	6 slices, peeled and minced
Spring onions (scallions)	2, minced

Method

- Clean chicken. Rub outside of chicken with dark soy sauce and inside with combined seasoning ingredients.

- Stuff chicken with chopped spring onions and Chinese angelica root or star anise. Seal cavity with a small bamboo or metal skewer. Set aside.

- Heat a wok and pour in coarse salt. Heat, stirring constantly for 20–25 minutes until salt is very hot. Cover wok.

- Wrap chicken with three layers of paper, one sheet at a time. Oil the top sheet with a little cooking oil.

- Make a well in the centre of the heated salt and place chicken in it. Cover wrapped chicken completely with salt. Cover wok and leave chicken to cook on moderate heat for 10 minutes. Remove from heat.

- Reheat salt until very hot, stirring constantly to ensure salt is evenly heated. Return wrapped chicken to wok, this time with the other side down.

- Cover with salt and cook for another 10–15 minutes over low heat.

- Meanwhile, prepare ginger and spring onion dip. Warm oil and add salt. Remove from heat and stir well. Pour oil over minced ginger and spring onion. Set aside.

- Remove chicken from heat and unwrap. Discard stuffing and cut chicken into bite-sized pieces. Serve hot with dip.

Tip:

Use an old wok to prepare this dish, as the salt will cause the wok to rust.

Pandan Chicken

Preparation time: 30 minutes   Cooking time: 10 minutes   Serves 6

Ingredients

Boneless chicken	500 g, cut into 6 x 2.5-cm pieces
Shallots	4, peeled
Young ginger	2-cm knob, peeled
Garlic	2 cloves, peeled
Lemongrass (*serai*)	1 stalk
Light soy sauce	3 tsp
Fish sauce	1 tsp
Worcestershire sauce	3 tsp
Salt	$^1/_2$ tsp
Ground white pepper	$^1/_2$ tsp
Chilli powder	2 tsp
Coconut cream	125 ml, from $^1/_2$ grated coconut and sufficient water
Screwpine (*pandan*) leaves	6, cleaned
Bamboo cocktail sticks	6
Cooking oil for deep-frying	

Method

- Rinse chicken pieces and dry well with paper towel.

- Blend (process) shallots, ginger, garlic and lemongrass together and mix with sauces, salt, pepper, chilli powder and coconut cream.

- Add chicken and mix well. Leave to marinate for at least 4 hours.

- Wrap each piece of chicken with a screwpine leaf and secure with a cocktail stick.

- Heat oil in a wok and deep-fry for 6–8 minutes or until chicken is cooked through.

- Drain and serve hot, allowing guests to unwrap the chicken on their own.

Paper-Wrapped Chicken with Mushrooms

Preparation time: 30 minutes   Cooking time: 40 minutes   Serves 10

Ingredients

Whole chicken	1, about 1.25 kg, cut into 10 large pieces
Spring onion (scallion)	1, chopped
Coriander (cilantro) leaves	2 sprigs, chopped
Dried Chinese mushrooms	20, soaked to soften
Oyster sauce	1 Tbsp
Sugar	$^1/_2$ tsp
Ground white pepper	$^1/_2$ tsp
Sesame oil	$^1/_2$ tsp
Dried scallops	2, crushed
Cooking oil	3 Tbsp + more for deep-frying
Ginger	2.5-cm knob, peeled and crushed
Chicken stock	125 ml (page 175) or water
Greaseproof paper	5 sheets, folded into ten 10 x 15-cm bags
Corn oil	1 Tbsp, mixed with 1 tsp sesame oil
Cucumber slices	

Seasoning

Salt	$^1/_2$ tsp
Ground white pepper	$^1/_2$ tsp
Five-spice powder	$^1/_2$ tsp
Sugar	1 tsp
Oyster sauce	2 Tbsp
Brandy	1 Tbsp
Ginger juice	$^1/_2$ Tbsp
Light soy sauce	$^1/_2$ Tbsp
Sesame oil	$^1/_2$ Tbsp
Cornflour (cornstarch)	1 Tbsp

Method

- Marinate chicken pieces in a bowl with combined seasoning ingredients and chopped spring onion and coriander. Leave for 3 hours or overnight in the refrigerator.

- Marinate mushrooms with oyster sauce, sugar, pepper and sesame oil for at least 1 hour.

- Steam dried scallops for 15 minutes or until soft. Shred with fingers and set aside.

- Heat cooking oil in a wok and fry ginger for 30 seconds. Add dried scallops and toss for a few seconds. Add marinated mushrooms and stir-fry for 1 minute. Pour in chicken stock or water and simmer over low heat for 8–10 minutes. Remove and leave to cool.

- Lightly grease the inside of each paper bag with corn oil and sesame oil mixture. Put a piece of chicken and two pieces of marinated mushrooms into each bag. Fold and seal the opening with a stapler.

- Heat oil for deep-frying in a wok. Deep-fry paper parcels for 7–8 minutes. Remove and drain.

- Arrange parcels on a serving dish and garnish with cucumber slices.

Herbal Beggar's Chicken

Preparation time: 40 minutes   Cooking time: 3 hours 15 minutes   Serves 8

Ingredients

Whole chicken	1, about 1.5 kg
Chinese rice wine	1 Tbsp
Chicken stock	3 Tbsp (page 175)
Plain (all-purpose) flour	1.5 kg
Salt	1 tsp
Water	875 ml
Greaseproof paper	2 sheets
Cling film or aluminium foil	

Seasoning A

Salt	$^1/_2$ tsp
Ground white pepper	$^1/_4$ tsp
Chinese rice wine	$^1/_2$ Tbsp
Sesame oil	$^1/_2$ Tbsp

Seasoning B

Sugar	$^1/_2$ Tbsp
Rock salt	$^1/_2$ tsp
Ground white pepper	$^1/_4$ tsp
Light soy sauce	1 Tbsp
Dark soy sauce	$^1/_2$ Tbsp
Chinese rice wine	$^1/_2$ Tbsp
Sesame oil	1 tsp
Shallot oil	2 tsp (page 175)

Herbs

Chinese angelica root (tong kwai)	10 g
Wolfberries (kei chi)	15 g
Polyconattum (yok chok)	20 g
Codonopsitis (tong sum)	20 g
Astragalus (pak kei)	3 pieces
Red dates (hung cho)	6, slit and stoned

Method

- Rub outside of chicken with combined seasoning A ingredients and inside with combined seasoning B ingredients.

- Rinse herbs, combine with rice wine and chicken stock and steam for 10–15 minutes. Stuff marinated chicken with steamed herbs and refrigerate for 3 hours.

- Mix flour with salt and water to form a stiff, pliable dough. Roll out into a rectangle big enough to wrap chicken. Set aside.

- Grease a sheet of greaseproof paper and wrap chicken. Cover over with cling wrap/aluminium foil and then wrap with remaining sheet of greaseproof paper.

- Wrap chicken parcel with dough. Place in a roasting pan and bake in a preheated oven at 190°C for 3 hours.

- Crack open dough and remove paper and cling film/aluminium foil. Serve hot.

Diced Chicken with Cashew Nuts

Preparation time: 20 minutes   Cooking time: 10 minutes   Serves 6

Ingredients

Chicken breast	1, cut into 1.25-cm cubes
Corn oil	4 Tbsp
Dried Chinese mushrooms	6, soaked to soften and diced
Onion	1, peeled and diced
Canned young corn	425 g, drained and diced
Green capsicums (bell pepper)	2, cored and diced
Carrot	1, medium, diced and parboiled
Roasted cashew nuts	90 g

Seasoning

Sugar	1 tsp
Sesame oil	1 tsp
Salt	1 tsp
Rice wine	1 tsp
Cornflour (cornstarch)	1 tsp
Corn oil	$1/2$ Tbsp

Sauce

Chicken stock	250 ml (page 175)
Oyster sauce	4 tsp
Light soy sauce	1 tsp
Sesame oil	1 tsp
Rice wine	1 tsp
Sugar	$1/2$ tsp
Salt	$1/2$ tsp
Cornflour (cornstarch)	1 Tbsp

Method

- Marinate chicken with combined seasoning ingredients for at least 30 minutes.

- Heat 1 Tbsp corn oil in a wok and stir-fry mushrooms for 1 minute. Dish out and stir-fry marinated chicken in the same oil until cooked. Remove and clean wok.

- Heat remaining corn oil in cleaned wok and fry onion until transparent and fragrant. Add mushrooms, cooked chicken and young corn. Stir-fry for 1–2 minutes.

- Add capsicum, carrot and lastly cashew nuts. Stir in combined sauce ingredients and mix well. Dish out and serve hot.

Soy Sauce Chicken

Preparation time: 15 minutes   Cooking time: 20 minutes   Serves 6

Ingredients

Chicken	600 g, cut into bite-size pieces
Cooking oil	2 Tbsp
Young ginger	5-cm knob, peeled and sliced
Dried Chinese mushrooms	8, soaked to soften
Chinese rice wine	1 Tbsp
Chicken stock	250 ml (page 175)
Spring onions (scallions)	2–3, cut into 2.5- cm lengths
Coriander (cilantro) leaves	3 sprigs, cut into 2.5- cm lengths
Cornflour (cornstarch)	2 tsp, mixed with 2 Tbsp water

Seasoning

Light soy sauce	2 tsp
Dark soy sauce	2 tsp
Oyster sauce	2 tsp
Sugar	$1^{1}/_{2}$ tsp
Salt	$^{1}/_{2}$ tsp
Ground white pepper	$^{1}/_{2}$ tsp

Method

- Marinate chicken in combined seasoning ingredients for at least 30 minutes.

- Heat oil in a deep saucepan and add ginger and Chinese mushrooms. Stir-fry for 2 minutes, then add marinated chicken. Cook, stirring frequently for 5 minutes or until chicken changes colour. Stir in Chinese rice wine and toss for a further 2 minutes.

- Add chicken stock and bring to the boil. Simmer on medium heat until chicken is cooked through and tender.

- Add spring onions and coriander and stir in cornflour mixture until sauce thickens. Serve hot.

Cencaluk Chicken

Preparation time: 15 minutes   Cooking time: 30 minutes   Serves 4

Ingredients

Chicken thighs	250 g, de-boned and cut into strips
Sugar	1 tsp
Cencaluk (fermented baby shrimps)	2 Tbsp
Cooking oil	2 Tbsp
Lemongrass (*serai*)	2 stems, crushed
Onions	2, peeled and cut into wedges
Garlic	2 cloves, peeled and minced
Water	125 ml
Dark soy sauce	1 tsp
Red chillies	2, sliced
Green chillies	2, sliced

Method

- Marinate chicken with sugar and salted prawns for 15 minutes.

- Heat oil in a wok and fry crushed lemongrass, onions and garlic until fragrant.

- Add chicken and stir-fry for another 2 minutes.

- Add water, dark soy sauce and chillies. Stir-fry until chicken is cooked and sauce is thickened. Serve hot.

Kung Po Chicken

Preparation time: 15 minutes   Cooking time: 15 minutes   Serves 4

Ingredients

Chicken breast	300 g, cut into 1-cm cubes
Cooking oil for deep-frying	
Garlic	2 cloves, peeled and chopped
Ginger	4 thin slices, peeled
Hot bean paste	1 Tbsp
Dried chillies	2, cut into 1-cm thick slices, rinsed
Red chilli	1, seeded and cut into 1-cm thick slices
Sichuan peppercorns (*fah chew*)	$^1/_2$ tsp
Roasted peanuts	50 g
Spring onions (scallion)	2, cut slantwise into 1-cm pieces

Seasoning

Light soy sauce	1 Tbsp
Dark soy sauce	1 tsp
Chinese rice wine	1 tsp
Sugar	1 tsp
Ground white pepper	a dash
Cornflour (cornstarch)	2 tsp

Stock

Chicken stock	75 ml (page 175)
Chinese rice wine	1 tsp
Sugar	$^1/_2$ tsp

Method

• Season chicken with combined seasoning ingredients for 30 minutes.

• Heat oil for deep-frying, reserving 1 Tbsp oil. Just before putting chicken into hot oil, stir reserved oil into chicken. Deep-fry oiled chicken for 15 seconds then drain and set aside.

• Leaving 1 Tbsp oil in wok, lightly brown garlic and ginger. Add hot bean paste and stir for 15 seconds.

• Add dried and red chillies and Sichuan pepper. Pour in combined stock ingredients. When it boils, return chicken to wok. Stir in peanuts and spring onions. Serve hot.

Braised Chicken Feet with Mushrooms

Preparation time: 15 minutes   Cooking time: 2 hours 15 minutes   Serves 8–10

Ingredients

Chicken feet	20, claws trimmed, chopped in half
Cooking oil for deep-frying	
Shallots	2, peeled and sliced
Garlic	3 cloves, peeled and minced
Star anise	2 petals
Sichuan peppercorns (*fah chew*)	1 heaped tsp
Dried Chinese mushrooms	6, soaked to soften

Seasoning

Ground white pepper	1 tsp
Light soy sauce	1 Tbsp
Dark soy sauce	1 tsp

Sauce

Chicken stock	375 ml (page 175)
Dark soy sauce	1 Tbsp
Light soy sauce	1 tsp
Salt	1 tsp
Sugar	1 tsp
Ground white pepper	$^{1}/_{2}$ tsp

Method

- Marinate chicken feet with combined seasoning ingredients for at least 1 hour.

- Heat wok with oil for deep-frying until hot. Add chicken feet and cover wok to prevent oil from splattering. Deep-fry chicken feet for 5 minutes or until golden brown. Drain and soak in cold water for 30 minutes. Drain.

- Leave 2 Tbsp of oil in wok and lightly brown shallots and garlic. Add star anise and Sichuan peppercorns and return chicken feet to wok. Toss briefly for 2 minutes.

- Transfer mixture into an electric crock pot and add combined sauce ingredients. Cook on high heat for 1 hour.

- Add mushrooms and continue to slow cook, stirring occasionally, for another hour or until chicken feet are tender and sauce thickens. Serve hot.

Tamarind Chicken (Ayam Sioh)

Preparation time: 15 minutes   Cooking time: 40 minutes   Serves 6–8

Ingredients

Whole chicken	1, about 1.5 kg, cut into 8 large pieces
Cooking oil	90 ml

Tamarind Sauce

Tamarind pulp	360 g, mixed with and 810 ml water and strained
Rice vinegar	1$^{1}/_{2}$ Tbsp
Dark soy sauce	2 Tbsp
Sugar	150 g
Salt	2 tsp
Ground coriander	3 Tbsp, roasted
Shallots	12, peeled and ground
Garlic	3 cloves, peeled and ground

Method

- Marinate chicken with combined tamarind sauce in a large bowl and leave overnight in the refrigerator.

- Pour tamarind sauce into a pot and bring to a slow boil. Add chicken pieces and boil over moderate heat for 20 minutes or until chicken is cooked and tender.

- Drain chicken in a colander and continue cooking sauce, stirring until thick. Remove from heat.

- Heat oil in a wok until hot and fry chicken for a few minutes until brown. Drain and arrange on a serving dish. Pour thick tamarind sauce over chicken. Serve hot or at room temperature.

Steamed Chicken Wings

Preparation time: 10 minutes   Cooking time: 12 minutes   Serves 6

Ingredients

Chicken wings	6 pairs, cut at joint
Cooking oil	1 Tbsp
Dried Chinese mushrooms	2, soaked to soften and sliced
Red chillies	2, seeded and sliced
Coriander (cilantro) leaves	1 sprig, chopped
Spring onion (scallion)	1, chopped

Seasoning

Light soy sauce	1 Tbsp
Oyster sauce	1 Tbsp
Cornflour (cornstarch)	2 tsp
Sugar	1 tsp
Dark soy sauce	1 tsp
Salt	$1/2$ tsp
Ground white pepper	$1/4$ tsp
Ginger	2.5-cm knob, peeled and minced

Method

- Wash and dry chicken wings thoroughly. Marinate with combined seasoning ingredients and oil. Leave for 1 hour.

- Place on a heatproof (flameproof) dish and sprinkle with sliced mushrooms and chillies. Steam over rapidly boiling water for 12 minutes.

- Remove and serve hot, sprinkled with chopped coriander leaves and spring onion.

Chicken and Bean Curd in Hoisin Sauce

Preparation time: 20 minutes   Cooking time: 15 minutes   Serves 4

Ingredients

Chicken thigh	1, skinned and cut into 2-cm pieces
Salt	$^1/_2$ tsp
Ground white pepper	$^1/_2$ tsp
Dried Chinese mushrooms	4, soaked to soften and halved
Sugar	$^1/_4$ tsp
Cooking oil	2 Tbsp
Garlic	3 cloves, peeled and minced
Ginger	4 thick slices, peeled
Firm bean curd (*tau korn*)	3 pieces, diced into 1.5-cm cubes
Green capsicum (bell pepper)	1, small, diced
Red chilli	1, seeded and diced
Cornflour (cornstarch)	1 tsp, mixed with 1 Tbsp water

Sauce

Chicken stock	125 ml (page 175)
Hoisin sauce	1 Tbsp
Oyster sauce	1 Tbsp
Salt	$^1/_4$ tsp
Sugar	$^1/_2$ tsp

Method

- Season chicken with half the salt and pepper. Set aside.

- Season mushrooms with remaining salt and pepper and sugar. Set aside.

- Heat oil in a wok and lightly brown garlic and ginger. Add chicken and cook for 1 minute. Add mushrooms and stir-fry until fragrant. Add bean curd and toss gently.

- Add capsicum and chilli and mix well. Combine sauce ingredients and add to wok. Bring to the boil and thicken with cornflour mixture. Serve hot.

Stewed Chicken (Ayam Pong Tay)

Preparation time: 15 minutes   Cooking time: 40 minutes   Serves 6

Ingredients

Chicken	1 kg or 600 g streaky pork
Salt	$^1/_2$ tsp
Cooking oil	90 ml
Shallots	180 g, peeled and ground
Garlic	3 bulbs, peeled and ground
Preserved soy beans (*tau cheo*)	2 Tbsp
Dried Chinese mushrooms	4–5, soaked to soften
Water	500 ml
Dark soy sauce	1 tsp
Potatoes	3, peeled and quartered
Salt	$^1/_2$ tsp

Method

- Cut chicken into small pieces. If using pork, cut into 5 x 2.5-cm pieces. Season meat with salt and leave aside.

- Heat oil in a wok and fry ground shallots and garlic for 2 minutes, then add preserved soy beans and fry over low heat until fragrant.

- Add mushrooms, then meat and stir-fry for a few minutes. Add water and dark soy sauce and bring to the boil. Lower heat and simmer, covered, for 15 minutes, then add potatoes and salt.

- Simmer gently for a further 12–15 minutes until meat is tender and sauce is quite thick. Serve hot.

Roasted Duck with Plum Sauce
(Pee Par Hup)

Preparation time: 5 minutes   Cooking time: 1 hour 25 minutes   Serves 8–10

Ingredients

Roasted duck	1
Cooking oil for deep-frying	
Sesame seeds	1 Tbsp, roasted
Coriander (cilantro) leaves	1 sprig, chopped
Tomatoes	2, sliced

Sauce

Tomato sauce	3 Tbsp
Chilli sauce	1 Tbsp
Plum sauce	1 Tbsp
Sugar	5 tsp
Salt	$^{1}/_{2}$ tsp
Sesame oil	2 tsp
A1 steak sauce	2 Tbsp
Worcestershire sauce	1 Tbsp
Hot water	75 ml
Cornflour (cornstarch)	1 tsp

Method

- Put roasted duck in a steamer over rapidly boiling water and steam for 1 hour. If preferred, duck can be steamed the night before.

- Make a cut lengthwise down breast of duck with a sharp cleaver but do not cut through.

- Heat oil for deep-frying in a wok until hot. Fry duck, turning over occasionally, for 15–20 minutes until skin is crisp and golden brown.

- Cut duck into serving-sized pieces and arrange neatly on a dish.

- Drain oil from wok, leaving a little to cook sauce. Heat oil and add combined sauce ingredients. Stir until sauce is thick. Spoon over duck and sprinkle with roasted sesame seeds. Serve hot, garnished with coriander leaves and tomatoes.

Claypot Ginger Duck

Preparation time: 20 minutes   Cooking time: 1 hour 30 minutes   Serves 8–10

Ingredients

Cooking oil	2 Tbsp
Young ginger	210 g, peeled and sliced
Garlic	7 cloves, peeled, finely minced
Fermented bean curd (*lam yee*)	1 piece
Hot soy bean garlic paste	2 Tbsp
Duck	1, about $2^3/_4$ kg, skinned, feet and neck removed, chopped into bite-sized pieces
Sugar	1 Tbsp
Dark soy sauce	1 Tbsp
Water	875 ml
Cornflour (cornstarch)	2 tsp, mixed with 2 Tbsp water
Spring onion (scallion)	1 Tbsp, chopped
Coriander (cilantro) leaves	1 Tbsp, chopped

Method

- Heat oil in a 10-cm wide claypot. Fry ginger pieces until fragrant. Add garlic and brown lightly.

- Add fermented bean curd and hot soy bean garlic paste and stir-fry until fragrant.

- Add duck and cook for 2 minutes. Add sugar and dark soy sauce. Toss to mix well.

- Add water and bring to the boil. Reduce heat and simmer, covered, for 1 hour or more until duck is tender and sauce is reduced. Stir frequently during simmering.

- Thicken with cornflour mixture and stir in chopped spring onion and coriander. Serve hot.

MEAT

Steamed Pork with Salted Fish

Preparation time: 15 minutes   Cooking time: 15 minutes   Serves 4

Ingredients

Belly pork	180 g, skinned and coarsely minced
Ginger	5 slices, peeled and shredded
Red chilli	1, sliced
Lime	1, small, juice extracted
Salted fish (threadfin)	45 g, thinly sliced

Seasoning

Ground white pepper	$^1/_4$ tsp
Sugar	$^1/_2$ tsp
Sesame oil	1 tsp
Light soy sauce	$^1/_2$ tsp
Cornflour (cornstarch)	1 tsp

Method

• Season pork with combined seasoning ingredients in a heatproof (flameproof) dish. Mix in ginger, chilli and lime juice and leave for 30 minutes.

• Spread salted fish on top of pork mixture and steam over rapidly boiling water for 15 minutes. Serve hot.

Bean Curd Wrapped Pork Roll (Lor Bak)

Preparation time: 20 minutes   Cooking time: 12 minutes   Serves 6

Ingredients

Pork	300 g, cut into 2 x 11.5-cm strips
Dried bean curd skin (*fu pei*)	6, about 20-cm square each
Egg white	$1/2$, beaten
Cooking oil for deep-frying	
Chilli sauce	

Seasoning

Onion	1, peeled and ground
Oyster sauce	2 tsp
Light soy sauce	2 tsp
Dark soy sauce	1 tsp
Sugar	1 tsp
Five-spice powder	1 tsp
Salt	$1/2$ tsp
Egg	1, beaten

Method

*   Marinate pork strips with combined seasoning ingredients for 2 hours or overnight in the refrigerator.

*   Spread out a square of bean curd skin and place 2 strips of meat lengthwise on sheet. Wrap and roll up like a spring roll. Seal edges with a little beaten egg white.

*   Prick bean curd skin with a needle to prevent air bubbles forming when frying. Repeat with remaining pork and bean curd skin sheets.

*   Heat oil for deep-frying until hot. Reduce heat and deep-fry bean curd rolls until golden brown. Drain from oil.

*   Cut into bite-sized pieces and serve with chilli sauce.

Five-Spice Meat Roll

Preparation time: 30 minutes   Cooking time: 20 minutes   Serves 6–8

Ingredients

Minced chicken	600 g
Small prawns (shrimps)	300 g, peeled, cleaned and minced
Crab meat	240 g
Carrot	10-cm piece, coarsely minced
Fresh water chestnuts	6, peeled and coarsely minced
Dried Chinese mushrooms	5, soaked to soften and coarsely minced
Spring onions (scallions)	2–3, chopped
Egg	$1/2$, beaten
Plain (all-purpose) flour	1 Tbsp
Dried bean curd skin (*fu pei*)	1 large sheet, cut into 30 x 12.5-cm pieces
Egg white	$1/2$, beaten
Cooking oil for deep-frying	

Seasoning

Five-spice powder	$1/2$ tsp
Salt	$1/2$ tsp
Ground white pepper	$1/2$ tsp
Light soy sauce	$1/2$ Tbsp
Sesame oil	$1/2$ Tbsp

Method

- Combine chicken, prawns, crab meat, carrot, water chestnuts, mushrooms and spring onions. Mix with seasoning ingredients, egg and plain flour. Leave for 1 hour.

- Put some marinated meat mixture in the centre of each bean curd sheet and roll up into rolls 4-cm in diameter. Seal edges with a little egg white. Repeat with remaining meat and bean curd skin sheets.

- Place rolls in a steamer over rapidly boiling water and steam for 12 minutes. Cut rolls into 2.5-cm slices with a sharp knife.

- Heat oil for deep-frying in a wok until hot and fry five-spice roll slices until light golden brown. Serve hot with chilli sauce.

Mutton Curry (Kari Kambing)

Preparation time: 30 minutes   Cooking time: 1 hour   Serves 8

Ingredients

Cooking oil	100 ml
Cinnamon stick	2.5-cm length
Cardamom	3 pods
Cloves	6
Star anise	2 petals
Mutton or beef	600 g, thinly sliced
Coconut milk	750 ml, from 1 grated coconut, squeezed first for coconut cream, then add sufficient water to extract coconut milk
Potatoes	4, peeled and quartered
Tomatoes	3, halved
Coconut cream	500 ml, from 1 grated coconut and sufficient water
Salt	$1\frac{1}{2}$ tsp

Curry Paste

Shallots	8, peeled
Garlic	3 cloves, peeled
Ginger	5-cm knob, peeled
Galangal	2.5-cm knob, peeled
Meat curry powder	5 Tbsp

Method

- Heat oil in a pot and fry whole spices for a few minutes.

- Combine curry paste ingredients and grind into a fine paste. Add curry paste to wok and stir-fry until fragrant and oil separates.

- Add meat and fry until well coated with ground ingredients.

- Add coconut milk and bring to the boil, then simmer gently for 40 minutes or until meat is almost tender.

- Add potatoes, then tomatoes. Add coconut cream and simmer until meat is tender and gravy is thick. Stir in salt and serve hot.

Red Curry (Daging Masak Merah)

Preparation time: 45 minutes   Cooking time: 1 hour   Serves 8

Ingredients

Beef	600 g, scored and cut into 4-cm cubes
Ginger	5-cm knob, peeled and ground
Turmeric	5-cm knob, peeled and ground
Cooking oil	120 ml
Shallots	450 g, peeled and sliced
Cashew nuts	120 g
Sultanas	90 g
Dried chillies	40, soaked to soften and ground
Water	1.25 litres
Jackfruit leaves (optional)	2–3
Evaporated milk	410 g (1 can)
Tomato puree	70 g ($^1/_2$ can)
Tomato sauce	4 Tbsp
Tamarind pulp	2 tsp, mixed with a little water and strained
Salt	2 tsp
Mint leaves	a few sprigs
Coriander (cilantro) leaves	2 sprigs, cut into 2.5-cm lengths
Spring onions (scallions)	2, cut into 2.5-cm lengths
Sugar	1 tsp

Method

- Marinate beef with ground ginger and turmeric and set aside.

- Heat oil in a wok and lightly brown shallots until crisp. Remove with a perforated ladle and set aside.

- Reheat oil and fry cashew nuts until lightly browned. Drain and set aside.

- Put sultanas into oil and fry for 1 minute. Remove and drain. Set aside.

- Add ground dried chillies and fry until oil separates. Dish out and leave aside.

- Return beef to wok and add water and jackfruit leaves if using. Bring to the boil then lower heat and simmer for 1 hour until beef is tender. Discard jackfruit leaves.

- Add crisp-fried shallots, cashew nuts, sultanas, ground chillies and all remaining ingredients. Simmer, stirring frequently, until gravy is thick and meat is tender. Serve hot.

Spicy Mutton Soup

Preparation time: 20 minutes   Cooking time: 2 hours 15 minutes   Serves 8

Ingredients

Mutton	1 kg, fatty streaks removed and cut into 2.5-cm cubes
Water	2.5 litres
Cinnamon stick	5-cm length
Cloves	8
Star anise	2
White peppercorns	1 tsp
Coriander seeds	$^1/_2$ tsp
Fennel seeds	$^1/_2$ tsp
Cumin seeds	$^1/_2$ tsp
Salt	2 tsp
Shallots	8, peeled, sliced and crisp-fried
Garlic	3 cloves, peeled and crisp-fried
Spring onions (scallions)	2, chopped

Method

- Put mutton and water in a pot and bring to the boil.

- Lightly crush spices and tie up securely in a piece of muslin. Drop spice bag into boiling soup. Lower heat and simmer gently for 2 hours until meat is tender.

- Skim off scum and add salt. Serve hot, garnished with fried shallots and garlic and spring onions.

SEAFOOD

Butter Prawns with Toasted Coconut

Preparation time: 15 minutes   Cooking time: 20 minutes   Serves 6

Ingredients

Large prawns (shrimps)	500 g, cleaned and feelers trimmed
Salt	$^1/_2$ tsp
Ground white pepper	$^1/_2$ tsp
Cooking oil for deep-frying	
Butter	90 g
Dry-roasted grated coconut	60 g, blended in electric blender
Sugar	2 tsp
Salt	$^1/_2$ tsp
Bird's eye chillies (*cili padi*)	10, finely sliced
Spring onions (scallions)	2, chopped
Coriander (cilantro) leaves	2 sprigs, chopped
Lime	1, small, juice extracted

Omelette

Eggs	2, beaten
Light soy sauce	1 tsp
Salt	$^1/_4$ tsp
Ground white pepper	$^1/_2$ tsp

Method

•   Season prawns with salt and pepper. Set aside.

•   Combine omelette ingredients in a bowl. Heat a flat-based non-stick pan and pour in one-third of mixture. Tilt pan around to create a thin omelette. Remove from heat and repeat process with remaining mixture. Chop omelettes up into fine strips. Set aside.

•   Heat oil for deep-frying and deep-fry prawns until just cooked. Drain.

•   Heat butter over low heat, add toasted coconut, sugar, salt and bird's eye chilli. Toss well and cook until fragrant. Add finely chopped omelette, spring onions, coriander leaves and lime juice.

•   Add prawns and toss until well coated with omelette mixture. Serve hot.

Chilli Cuttlefish (Dry Sambal Sotong)

Preparation time: 20 minutes   Cooking time: 15 minutes   Serves 6

Ingredients

Pre-soaked cuttlefish (*sotong kembang*)	600 g
Cooking oil	75 ml
Onions	2, peeled and sliced
Water	80 ml
Tomatoes	2, each cut into 8 wedges
Sugar	2 tsp
Salt	1 tsp
Tamarind pulp	1 Tbsp, mixed with 125 ml water and strained

Chilli Paste

Dried chillies	15, cut and seeded
Red chillies	5, cut and seeded
Shallots	12, peeled and sliced
Garlic	2 cloves, peeled and sliced
Dried shrimp paste (*belachan*) granules	1 Tbsp
Turmeric	2-cm knob, peeled

Method

- Cut cuttlefish into bite-sized pieces and set aside.

- Combine chilli paste ingredients and blend (process) until fine.

- Heat oil in a wok and cook onions until soft. Add chilli paste and stir-fry over low heat until oil separates. Add water and bring to the boil.

- Add tomatoes, sugar and salt. Stir in cuttlefish and cook for 3 minutes.

- Pour in tamarind water and cook for 2–3 minutes more. Adjust seasoning to taste and serve hot.

Sambal Fish with Bilimbi

Preparation time: 10 minutes   Cooking time: 15 minutes   Serves 4

Ingredients

Spanish mackerel (*ikan tenggiri*)	450 g
Salt	2 tsp
Bilimbi (*belimbing asam*)	8
Cooking oil	3 Tbsp
Red chillies	2, seeded and sliced slantwise
Lemongrass (*serai*)	1 stalk, crushed
Coconut milk	250 ml, from $^1/_2$ grated coconut and sufficient water
Sugar	1 tsp
Salt	$^1/_2$ tsp

Paste

Red chillies	6, cut and seeded
Dried chillies	10, soaked to soften and cut
Shallots	10, peeled and cut
Candlenuts (*buah keras*)	3
Dried shrimp paste (*belachan*)	2.5 x 1.5-cm piece

Method

- Season fish with 1 tsp salt for 10 minutes. Set aside.

- Rub bilimbi with remaining salt and set aside.

- Combine paste ingredients and blend (process) until fine.

- Heat oil in a wok and fry paste, red sliced chillies and lemongrass until fragrant and oil separates.

- Pour in coconut milk, bilimbi, sugar and salt and bring to a slow boil. Add fish and simmer for 5 minutes until cooked. Serve hot.

Note:

If bilimbi is not available, use 1 Tbsp lemon juice as substitute.

Teochew Steamed Fish

Preparation time: 15 minutes   Cooking time: 18 minutes   Serves 5–6

Ingredients

Whole fish (threadfin or pomfret)	600–900 g
Salt	$1^{1}/_{2}$ tsp
Ground white pepper	1 tsp
Salted cabbage	120 g, soaked and sliced
Dried Chinese mushrooms	4, soaked to soften and cut into strips
Chicken or pork	90 g, cut into strips
Ginger	4-cm knob, peeled and cut into strips
Red chillies	2, cut into strips
Pickled sour plums	2
Sesame oil	1 tsp
Water	125 ml
Cooking oil	3 Tbsp
Shallots	3–4, peeled and sliced
Spring onions (scallions)	2, cut into 5–cm lengths
Coriander (cilantro) leaves	2 sprigs, cut into 5–cm lengths

Method

- Clean fish thoroughly and rub with salt and pepper. Place on a heatproof (flameproof) dish and arrange salted cabbage, mushrooms, chicken or pork, ginger and chillies over fish.

- Lightly squeeze sour plums over fish and place beside fish. Add sesame oil and water.

- Place dish in a steamer over rapidly boiling water and steam for 15 minutes.

- Meanwhile, heat cooking oil in a wok and fry shallots until lightly browned.

- When fish is cooked, pour oil and shallots over fish. Serve garnished with spring onions and coriander leaves.

Braised Fish Head (Hoong Siew Yee Tau)

Preparation time: 30 minutes   Cooking time: 30 minutes   Serves 6

Ingredients

Fish head (garoupa, red snapper or threadfin)	1, about 1 kg
Ginger juice	1 Tbsp
Light soy sauce	1/2 Tbsp
Chicken	100 g, shredded
Salt	1/4 tsp
Ground white pepper	1/4 tsp
Cornflour (cornstarch)	3 Tbsp
Oil for deep-frying	
Ginger	5 slices, peeled and shredded
Garlic	3 cloves, peeled and sliced
Shallot	1, peeled and sliced
Dried Chinese mushrooms	4, soaked to soften and halved
Carrots	120 g, sliced and parboiled
Young corns	6, each halved
Green capsicum (bell pepper) 1/2 , cut into 2-cm pieces	
Chinese rice wine	1/2 Tbsp
Cornflour (cornstarch) thickener	1 tsp cornflour, mixed with 1 Tbsp water
Egg white	1, lightly beaten
Spring onion (scallion)	1, cut into 2.5-cm lengths
Coriander (cilantro) leaves	1 sprig, cut into 2.5-cm lengths
Red chilli	1, cut into strips

Sauce

Chicken stock	250 ml (page 175)
Light soy sauce	1 Tbsp
Dark soy sauce	1 tsp
Chinese rice wine	1 tsp
Sesame oil	1 tsp
Sugar	1 tsp
Ground white pepper	1 tsp
Salt	1/2 tsp

Method

- Clean fish head and halve. Season with ginger juice and light soy sauce for 30 minutes. Marinate shredded chicken with salt and pepper.

- Heat oil for deep-frying in a wok until hot. Coat fish with cornflour and deep-fry for 3–5 minutes. Remove and drain from oil.

- Heat a clean wok with 3 Tbsp oil and lightly brown half the ginger shreds, garlic and shallot. Add mushrooms and stir-fry for 1 minute until fragrant.

- Add shredded chicken and when it changes colour, add carrots, young corns and capsicum. Stir-fry for 1 minute, then sprinkle in wine.

- Combine sauce ingredients and pour into wok. Bring to the boil. Place fish head in and reduce heat. Cover wok and simmer for 5 minutes. Remove fish head and arrange on a serving dish.

- Thicken sauce in wok with cornflour mixture and beaten egg white. Stir in remaining ginger shreds, spring onion, coriander and chilli. Pour sauce over fish head and serve hot.

Tamarind Squid

Preparation time: 15 minutes   Cooking time: 20 minutes   Serves 4

Ingredients

Squid (*sotong*)	450 g, small or medium-sized
Tamarind pulp	3 Tbsp, mixed with 625 ml water and strained
Dried shrimp paste (*belachan*)	1.25-cm square
Sugar	2 tsp
Salt	1 tsp
Dried sour fruit (*asam gelugur*)	3 pieces
Shallots	12, peeled and sliced
Lemongrass (*serai*)	2 stalks, crushed
Red chillies	4, split lengthwise, stems retained
Green chillies	4, split lengthwise, stems retained

Method

- Wash and remove ink sac from squid. Set aside.

- Put tamarind juice, dried shrimp paste, sugar, salt, tamarind skin, shallots and lemongrass into a pot.

- Bring to the boil then add red and green chillies. Simmer gently for 10 minutes.

- Add squid and boil for 3–4 minutes until just cooked. Serve hot.

Fresh Scallops on Bean Curd

Preparation time: 20 minutes   Cooking time: 15 minutes   Serves 8

Ingredients

Fresh scallops	12
Chicken meat	150 g, minced
Prawns (shrimps)	150 g, small, peeled and minced
Water chestnuts	2, peeled and finely chopped
Red chilli	1, finely chopped
Spring onion (scallion)	1, finely chopped
Coriander (cilantro) leaves	1 sprig, finely chopped
Soft bean curd (*taufu*)	600 g, cut to obtain 12 regular pieces
Cooking oil	1 Tbsp
Cornflour (cornstarch)	1 tsp, mixed with 1 Tbsp water

Seasoning A

Salt	$^1/_4$ tsp
Ground white pepper	$^1/_4$ tsp
Sugar	$^1/_4$ tsp
Cornflour (cornstarch)	$^1/_4$ tsp

Seasoning B

Sesame oil	1 tsp
Light soy sauce	$^1/_2$ tsp
Chinese rice wine	$^1/_2$ tsp
Salt	$^1/_2$ tsp
Ground white pepper	$^1/_4$ tsp
Cornflour (cornstarch)	1 tsp

Sauce

Chicken stock	125 ml (page 175)
Light soy sauce	1 tsp
Chinese rice wine	1 tsp
Oyster sauce	1 tsp
Sugar	$^1/_2$ tsp
Salt	$^1/_4$ tsp
Ground white pepper	$^1/_4$ tsp

Method

- Combine ingredients for Seasoning A and put scallops in to marinate.

- Combine ingredients for Seasoning B and marinate minced chicken and prawns. Add finely chopped ingredients and set aside for 30 minutes.

- Using a 2.5-cm wide biscuit cutter, carefully stamp out the centre of each piece of bean curd, or use a knife to hollow out the centre. Gently lift and arrange hollowed-out bean curd pieces on a heatproof dish. (You may refrigerate the cut-out portions of bean curd in a bowl of water and use in soups instead of discarding them).

- Carefully fill the hollow of each bean curd piece with 1 tsp of minced meat and prawn mixture. Top with a scallop and steam over rapidly boiling water for 8 minutes.

- Meanwhile combine sauce ingredients in a bowl. Remove heatproof dish from steamer and pour resulting juices into sauce. Mix well.

- Heat oil in a wok and boil sauce. When it begins to boil, thicken with cornflour. Pour over steamed bean curd and serve hot.

Fried Prawns with Stink Beans
(Udang Tumis Petai)

Preparation time: 30 minutes   Cooking time: 15 minutes   Serves 6

Ingredients

Galangal	2.5-cm knob, peeled
Turmeric	2.5-cm knob, peeled
Roasted cashew nuts	10
Lemongrass (*serai*)	4 stalks
Dried chillies	20, soaked to soften
Red chillies	5
Bird's eye chillies (*cili padi*)	5
Shallots	240 g, peeled
Garlic	2 cloves, peeled
Dried shrimp paste (*belachan*)	4 x 2.5-cm piece
Small prawns (shrimps)	600 g, peeled and cleaned
Cooking oil	6 Tbsp
Tamarind pulp	1 heaped Tbsp, mixed with 125 ml water and strained
Stink beans (*petai*)	15 pods, removed from pods and skinned
Sugar	1 tsp
Salt	1$\frac{1}{2}$ tsp

Method

- Combine galingale, turmeric, cashew nuts and lemongrass and blend (process) into a paste. Set aside.

- Combine chillies, shallots, garlic and dried shrimp and blend into a paste. Set aside.

- Heat oil in a wok and fry ground galingale paste until fragrant. Add ground chilli paste and fry over low heat until fragrant and oil separates.

- Add prawns and stir-fry for a few minutes, taking care not to overcook prawns. Add tamarind juice and bring to a slow boil.

- Add stink beans and stir in sugar and salt. Stir-fry for 2 minutes. Dish out and serve hot.

EGGS & BEAN CURD

Dried Radish Omelette

Preparation time: 15 minutes   Cooking time: 10 minutes   Serves 4

Ingredients

Eggs	3
Spring onion (scallion)	1, chopped
Cooking oil	2 Tbsp
Garlic	2 cloves, peeled and minced
Dried salted radish (*choy poh*)	45 g, soaked for 10 minutes, drained and minced

Seasoning

Light soy sauce	1 tsp
Sugar	$1/2$ tsp
Sesame oil	$1/2$ tsp
Ground white pepper	$1/4$ tsp

Method

- Beat eggs well with a fork and add seasoning ingredients and spring onion. Mix well and set aside.

- Heat a flat pan or wok with half the oil and stir-fry garlic and minced dried radish for 1–2 minutes over low heat. Remove and stir into egg mixture.

- Heat pan or wok again with remaining oil until hot. Pour in egg mixture and cook over low heat until lightly browned. Turn over and cook other side until lightly browned. Remove from heat and cut in slices or leave whole. Serve hot.

Herbal Tea Eggs

Preparation time: 15 minutes   Cooking time: 3–3 hours 30 minutes   Makes 12

Ingredients

Eggs	12, at room temperature
Chinese tea leaves	4 Tbsp
Dark soy sauce	3 Tbsp
Salt	1 Tbsp
Sugar	$1/2$ tsp
Chinese angelica root (*tong kwai*)	15 g
Codonopsis pilosula (*dong sum*)	10 g
Astragalus (*pak kei*)	10 g
Polyconattum (*yok chok*)	10 g
Medlar seeds/wolfberries (*kei chi*)	5 g

Method

- Put eggs in a large pot and add water to cover. Bring to the boil then reduce heat and simmer for 15 minutes.

- Drain eggs and allow to cool. Gently tap eggs with the back of a spoon to crack shells, but do not remove shells.

- Return eggs to pot and add water to cover eggs completely.

- Stir in remaining ingredients and bring to the boil. Either reduce heat to very low and simmer for 3 hours or place in a crock pot for $3^1/2$ hours.

- Drain and leave to cool. Shell eggs and serve whole or cut in wedges.

Claypot Bean Curd with Mushrooms

Preparation time: 15 minutes   Cooking time: 15 minutes   Serves 4

Ingredients

Prawns (shrimps)	90 g, small, peeled and deveined
Salt	1/4 tsp
Sugar	1/4 tsp
Ground white pepper	1/4 tsp
Cooking oil	1/2 Tbsp
Chinese rice wine	1 Tbsp
Fresh Shiitake mushrooms	3, rinsed and sliced
Silken soft bean curd (*taufu*)	300 g, cut into small cubes
Potato flour	1 1/2 Tbsp, mixed with 3 Tbsp water
Egg whites	2, lightly beaten with 1 Tbsp water
Shallot oil	1/2 Tbsp (page 175)
Black vinegar	a dash
Spring onion (scallion)	1/2, chopped

Stock

Chicken stock	625 ml (page 175)
Salt	1 tsp
Light soy sauce	2 tsp
Ground white pepper	1/4 tsp

Method

- Season prawns with salt, sugar and pepper.

- Combine stock ingredients in a bowl.

- Heat oil in a medium-sized claypot and add wine and stock. Bring to the boil and stir in mushrooms, prawns and bean curd cubes.

- Allow sauce to come to the boil again, then thicken with potato flour mixture.

- Gradually stir in beaten egg white and water mixture, then shallot oil.

- Serve with a dash of black vinegar and garnish with chopped spring onion.

Steamed Bean Curd with Chicken, Salted and Century Eggs

Preparation time: 20 minutes   Cooking time: 15 minutes   Serves 4

Ingredients

Silken soft bean curd (taufu)	600 g
Salt	a pinch
Shallot oil	2 tsp (page 175)
Salted egg	1, boiled, white discarded and yolk chopped
Cooking oil	1 Tbsp
Garlic	2 cloves, peeled and finely minced
Canned pickled cabbage	50 g, drained and cut into 1-cm pieces
Minced chicken	120 g, seasoned with a pinch each of salt and ground white pepper
Century egg	1, peeled, yolk discarded and translucent portion diced
Potato flour	2 tsp, mixed with 2 Tbsp water

Sauce

Chicken stock	250 ml (page 175)
Light soy sauce	2 tsp
Oyster sauce	1 tsp
Sugar	$^{1}/_{2}$ tsp
Salt	$^{1}/_{2}$ tsp
Sesame oil	$^{1}/_{2}$ tsp

Method

- Carefully place bean curd on a heatproof (flameproof) dish. Season with salt and shallot oil.

- Sprinkle salted egg yolk over bean curd. Steam over rapidly boiling water for 10 minutes.

- Meanwhile, heat cooking oil in wok and lightly brown garlic. Add pickled vegetables and cook for 30 seconds. Add seasoned minced chicken and stir-fry until chicken changes colour.

- Pour in sauce ingredients and bring to a quick boil. Add century egg then thicken with potato flour mixture.

- Carefully remove bean curd from steamer and drain off excess water. Pour thickened sauce over bean curd. Serve hot.

Pickled Vegetable, Chicken and Bean Curd Soup

Preparation time: 15 minutes   Cooking time: 15 minutes   Serves 4

Ingredients

Minced chicken	100 g
Salt	1^1/$_2$ tsp
Ground white pepper	^{1}/$_4$ tsp
Potato flour	1 tsp
Cooking oil	^{1}/$_2$ Tbsp
Garlic	1 clove, peeled and minced
Pickled vegetables (*harm choy*)	35 g, rinsed
Chicken stock	1 litre (page 175)
Silken soft bean curd (*taufu*)	300 g, diced
Spring onion (scallion)	1, chopped

Method

- Season chicken with a pinch of salt, pepper and potato flour and set aside for 15 minutes.

- Heat oil in a soup pot and stir-fry garlic and pickled vegetables until fragrant. Add seasoned chicken and cook until it changes colour.

- Add chicken stock and remaining salt. Stir and bring to the boil. Reduce heat and simmer for 2–3 minutes.

- Add bean curd and when stock boils again, sprinkle in chopped spring onion. Serve hot.

RICE & NOODLES

Fried Rice with Chicken and Pineapple

Preparation time: 20 minutes   Cooking time: 15 minutes   Serves 2

Ingredients

Chicken	120 g, diced
Salt	1 tsp
Ground white pepper	$^3/_4$ tsp
Cooking oil	2 Tbsp
Garlic	1 clove, peeled and minced
Shallots	2, peeled and sliced
Cooked rice	360 g, preferably 1 day old, loosened
Ham	2 slices, cut into strips
Carrot	60 g, diced and parboiled
Frozen green peas	1 Tbsp, defrosted
Fresh or canned pineapple	90 g, diced
Light soy sauce	1 Tbsp
Red chilli	1, chopped
Spring onion (scallion)	1, chopped
Coriander (cilantro) leaves	1 sprig, chopped

Method

- Marinate chicken with half the salt and a pinch of pepper for 15 minutes.

- Heat oil in a wok until hot and lightly brown garlic and shallots. Add chicken and stir-fry until meat changes colour.

- Add rice and toss briefly, breaking up any lumps. Add ham, carrot, green peas and pineapple and mix well.

- Add 1 tsp light soy sauce, remaining salt and pepper and stir-fry again for 1–2 minutes. Sprinkle in chopped chilli, spring onion and coriander leaves. Serve hot with a curry dish, if preferred.

Fragrant Herb Rice (Nasi Ulam)

Preparation time: 30 minutes   Cooking time: 30 minutes   Serves 8

Ingredients

Sambal

Red chillies	10
Shallots	5, peeled
Ginger	1.25-cm knob, peeled
Coconut cream	250 ml, from 1 grated coconut and sufficient water
Lemongrass (*serai*)	1 stalk, lightly crushed
Salt	$^1/_4$ tsp
Tamarind pulp	1 tsp, mixed with 2 Tbsp water and strained

Chubb mackerel (*ikan kembung*)	3, grilled, deboned and flesh ground
Turmeric leaves (*daun kunyit*)	5, finely sliced
Polygonum leaves (*daun kesum*)	4 sprigs, finely sliced
Basil leaves	4 stalks, finely sliced
Sweet basil (*selasih*) leaves	5 stalks, finely sliced
Watercress	4 stalks, finely sliced
Lesser galangal (*cekur*) leaves	3, fincly sliced
Kaffir lime leaves (*daun limau purut*)	3, finely sliced
Lettuce leaves	3, finely sliced
Cashew nut leaves (optional)	4, finely sliced
Lemongrass (*serai*)	2 stalks, tender central portion finely sliced
Shallots	6, peeled, finely sliced
Torch ginger flower (*bunga kantan*)	1, finely sliced
Green chillies	3, finely sliced
Grated skinned coconut	$^1/_2$ coconut, dry-roasted
Lime	1, large, juice extracted
Salt	1 tsp
Cooked rice	1.5 kg

Method

- Prepare sambal. Blend (process) chillies, shallots and ginger until fine. Combine ground ingredients with coconut cream, lemongrass, salt and tamarind juice and simmer over low heat. Stir until sauce is thick and oil separates. Set aside.

- Combine ground fish with the finely sliced ingredients and roasted grated coconut.

- Heat a wok without oil. When hot, turn off heat and add combined fish and sliced ingredients, lime juice and salt. Mix well. Transfer to a serving dish.

- To serve Nasi Ulam, ladle a portion of rice onto a plate, top with required amount of combined fish and sliced ingredients and sambal. Mix well and serve.

Fragrant Yam Rice

Preparation time: 20 minutes   Cooking time: 45 minutes   Serves 4

Ingredients

Chicken meat	300 g, cut into 2.5-cm pieces
Cooking oil	3 Tbsp + more for deep-frying
Yam	350 g, cut into 1.5-cm cubes
Shallots	6, peeled and sliced
Dried prawns (shrimps)	60 g, soaked for 15 minutes and drained
Rice	300 g, washed and drained
Light soy sauce	2 tsp
Chicken stock	875 ml (page 175)
Spring onion (scallion)	1, chopped
Red chilli	1, sliced

Seasoning

Salt	$^1/_2$ tsp
Sugar	$^1/_2$ tsp
Ground white pepper	$^1/_4$ tsp
Light soy sauce	1 tsp
Dark soy sauce	$^1/_2$ tsp
Sesame oil	1 tsp
Chinese rice wine	1 tsp
Cornflour (cornstarch)	1 tsp

Method

- Marinate chicken with combined seasoning ingredients and set aside.

- Heat oil for deep-frying and fry yam cubes for 8–10 minutes until just cooked. Drain from oil and set aside.

- Using the same oil, fry shallots until golden. Drain and set aside for garnishing.

- Remove all but 3 Tbsp oil and stir-fry prawns until fragrant. Dish out and set aside.

- Stir-fry rice in the same oil for 1–2 minutes. Stir in light soy sauce. Remove from heat and transfer rice to a rice cooker. Pour in chicken stock and switch on rice cooker to cook rice.

- When stock comes to a boil, add yam and chicken. Let rice cook until done. Garnish with shallot crisps, spring onion before serving.

Fried Rice Cake (Chao Ko)

Preparation time: 30 minutes   Cooking time: 1 hour   Serves 4–5

Ingredients

Shallot oil	2 Tbsp (page 175)
Rice cake	350 g, cut into 2-cm cubes (page 175)
Chopped garlic	1 heaped Tbsp
Dried salted radish (*choy poh*)	1 heaped Tbsp, rinsed and finely chopped
Chilli paste	1 Tbsp (page 175)
Bean sprouts	125 g, tailed
Chives (*kucai*)	75 g, cut into 3-cm lengths

Sauce

Fish sauce	1 Tbsp
Dark soy sauce	$\frac{1}{2}$ Tbsp
Sugar	$\frac{1}{2}$ tsp
Ground white pepper	a dash
Salt	a pinch
Eggs	2, beaten

Method

- Heat 1 Tbsp shallot oil in a non-stick wok over high heat until hot. Fry rice cubes until lightly golden. Remove from wok and set aside.

- Add remaining shallot oil and lightly brown garlic. Add dried salted radish and toss until fragrant.

- Add chilli paste and fry for 30 seconds. Add bean sprouts and toss well for a few seconds, then add chives.

- Pour in combined sauce ingredients and mix well. Return fried rice cubes to wok.

- Toss quickly and add beaten eggs, stirring until eggs are set. Serve hot.

Fried Mee Sua

Preparation time: 30 minutes   Cooking time: 15 minutes   Serves 5

Ingredients

Cooking oil for deep-frying	
Fine rice vermicelli (*mee sua*)	300 g, left unwashed
Bean sprouts	450 g
Water	1.5 litres
Shallots	5, peeled and sliced
Garlic	4 cloves, peeled and minced
Chicken or pork	150 g, cut into strips
Small prawns (shrimps)	300 g, peeled and cleaned
Salt	1 tsp
Ground white pepper	1 tsp
Chicken stock	750 ml (page 175)
Flowering cabbage (*choy sum*)	4 stalks, cut into 5-cm lengths
Light soy sauce	2 Tbsp
Spring onions (scallions)	2, cut into 2.5- cm lengths
Coriander (cilantro) leaves	1 sprig, cut into 2.5-cm lengths

Method

- Heat oil for deep-frying in a wok until hot. Add vermicelli, a bundle at a time, and fry, turning over very quickly with chopsticks until light golden. Vermicelli will sizzle in hot oil. Remove as soon as it stops sizzling. This takes only 15 seconds. Drain in a colander.

- Drain and reserve oil, leaving 3 Tbsp in wok and fry bean sprouts fry for 1 minute. Remove from heat and set aside.

- Bring water to the boil in a pot and add fried vermicelli. Cook for 1–2 minutes until soft. Immediately pour vermicelli into a colander and drain well.

- Heat 3 Tbsp reserved oil in wok and brown shallots and garlic. Add chicken or pork and stir-fry for 2 minutes, then add prawns, salt and pepper. When cooked, dish out and set aside.

- Pour chicken stock into wok and bring to the boil. Throw in flowering cabbage stems, then add light soy sauce and cook for 1 minute. Add flowering cabbage leaves, vermicelli, bean sprouts, fried chicken or pork and prawns, and mix.

- Throw in spring onions and coriander leaves. Serve hot with sliced red chillies in light soy sauce or chilli paste (page 175).

Fried Flat Rice Noodles with Beef

Preparation time: 30 minutes   Cooking time: 25 minutes   Serves 2

Ingredients

Beef	120 g, thinly sliced
Cooking oil	90 ml
Salt	$^1/_2$ tsp
Flowering cabbage (*choy sum*)	5 stalks, both ends trimmed
Fresh flat rice noodles	300 g, strands loosened
Light soy sauce	1 Tbsp, mixed with 1 Tbsp water
Bean sprouts	100 g
Spring onion (scallion)	1, cut into 2.5-cm lengths
Coriander (cilantro) leaves	1 sprig, cut into 2.5-cm lengths

Seasoning

Bicarbonate of soda	$^1/_3$ tsp
Ginger juice	2 tsp
Salt	$^1/_2$ tsp
Sugar	$^1/_4$ tsp
Cornflour (cornstarch)	2 tsp

Sauce

Chicken stock	5 Tbsp (page 175)
Light soy sauce	$^1/_2$ tsp
Dark soy sauce	2 tsp
Cornflour (cornstarch)	3 tsp

Method

- Marinate beef with combined seasoning ingredients except cooking oil. Mix well then add 1 Tbsp oil. Leave for at least 20 minutes.

- Bring half a saucepan of water to the boil. Add 1 Tbsp oil and salt. Scald flowering cabbage until just cooked. Drain well and arrange on a dish. Turn off heat and scald beef in same saucepan of water. Allow to soak for 1 minute. Skim off scum from surface, drain meat and set aside.

- Heat 1 Tbsp oil in a wok and tilt wok around to coat it in oil. Discard excess oil and add rice noodles. Toss noodles in hot wok for 2 minutes.

- Add light soy sauce and water mixture and stir-fry until well mixed. Remove and place noodles on flowering cabbage.

- Reheat wok with 1 Tbsp oil and stir-fry bean sprouts for 30 seconds. Remove and place over fried rice noodles.

- Clean wok and reheat with 1 Tbsp oil. Add combined sauce ingredients and add beef, then spring onion and coriander leaves. Toss quickly before adding remaining cooking oil. Mix well.

- Pour beef mixture over noodles and serve hot with cut red chillies in light soy sauce or chilli paste (page 175).

Fried Sar Ho Fun with Cockles

Preparation time: 20 minutes   Cooking time: 7 minutes   Serves 3

Ingredients

Cockles	300 g
Prawns (shrimps)	150 g, peeled and cleaned
Salt	$1/2$ tsp
Ground white pepper	$1/4$ tsp
Cooking oil	4 Tbsp
Garlic	3 cloves, peeled
Fresh flat rice noodles	600 g
Bean sprouts	150 g, tailed
Dark soy sauce	1 Tbsp
Light soy sauce	2 Tbsp
Eggs	2, lightly beaten
Water	4 Tbsp
Ground white pepper	a dash

Method

- Pour boiling water over cockles and drain immediately. Remove flesh from shells. Season prawns with salt and pepper and set aside.

- Heat three quarters of the oil in a wok until smoking hot. Add garlic and prawns and stir-fry quickly over high heat. Place noodles in and stir-fry for 1–2 minutes before adding bean sprouts. Stir to mix and add combined dark and light soy sauce. Stir-fry for 1 minute.

- Push noodles to one side of wok and add remaining oil. Pour in eggs, leave for 30 seconds to set then stir-fry together with noodles and bean sprouts.

- Sprinkle water over noodles while stirring. Lastly, add cockles and toss for 30 seconds. Remove from heat and serve hot, sprinkled with a dash of pepper.

Fried and Braised Noodles (Char Choo Mee)

Preparation time: 20 minutes   Cooking time: 20 minutes   Serves 4

Ingredients

Chicken meat	150 g skinned and sliced
Salt	1$^1/_2$ tsp
Ground white pepper	$^1/_4$ tsp
Fresh yellow noodles	500 g
Cooking oil	2 Tbsp
Shallots	2, peeled and sliced
Garlic	3 cloves, peeled and minced
Chicken stock	700 ml (page 175)
Dark soy sauce	$^1/_2$ tsp
Light soy sauce	1 Tbsp
Prawns (shrimps)	8, medium–large, eyes and feelers trimmed
Pre-fried bean curd (*chow taufu*)	20 pieces
Flowering cabbage (*choy sum*)	150 g
Spring onion (scallion)	1, chopped

Method

*   Season chicken with $^1/_2$ tsp salt and pepper and set aside for 15 minutes.

*   Bring a large saucepan of water to the boil and scald noodles for a few seconds. Drain well and set aside.

*   Heat oil in a wok and lightly brown shallots and garlic. Add noodles and remaining salt. Fry over high heat for 3–5 minutes or until noodles are half-cooked.

*   Pour in chicken stock, add dark and light soy sauces and stir well. When stock begins to boil, add chicken, prawns, bean curd and vegetables. Cover and simmer for 5 minutes.

*   Dish out and serve hot, garnished with chopped spring onion.

Fried Rice Noodles (Chao Loh Shee Fun)

Preparation time: 20 minutes   Cooking time: 20 minutes   Serves 4

Ingredients

Cooking oil	1½ Tbsp
Fresh short round rice noodles	600 g
Shallots	3, peeled and sliced
Garlic	3 cloves, peeled and finely minced
Dried Chinese mushrooms	3, soaked to soften and diced
Chicken thigh	1, skinned, diced and seasoned with salt and ground white pepper
Smoked turkey bacon (ham)	75 g, diced
Mustard green (*kai choy*) stems	3–4, cut into short lengths
Chinese rice wine	1 Tbsp
Pre-fried bean curd (*chow taufu*)	8 pieces, diced
Bean sprouts	200 g
Chicken stock	3 Tbsp (page 175)

Sauce

Light soy sauce	1 Tbsp
Dark soy sauce	1 Tbsp
Sweet black sauce	1 Tbsp
Sugar	½ tsp
Salt	½ tsp
Ground white pepper	¼ tsp

Method

- Add ½ Tbsp oil to a pot of boiling water and scald rice noodles for 1 minute.

- Heat remaining oil in a wok and lightly brown shallots and garlic.

- Add mushrooms and chicken and stir-fry briskly. When chicken changes colour, add turkey bacon (ham) and toss for a few seconds. Add mustard greens and Chinese rice wine. Add bean curd and bean sprouts and toss briefly.

- Add combined sauce ingredients and then the scalded noodles. Continue to stir-fry for 2–3 minutes. Stir in chicken stock and fry until noodles are slightly dry. Remove to a serving dish and serve hot.

Nasi Minyak

Preparation time: 15 minutes   Cooking time: 25 minutes   Serves 4

Ingredients

Rice	450 g
Ghee (clarified butter)	60 g
Shallots	6, peeled and sliced
Garlic	2 cloves, peeled and sliced
Ginger	1.25-cm knob, peeled and shredded
Cinnamon stick	2.5-cm length
Cloves	3
Cardamom	3 pods
Star anise	1
Water	680 ml
Screwpine (pandan) leaves	3, knotted
Evaporated milk	3 Tbsp
Salt	1 heaped tsp
Raisins	90 g
Crisp-fried shallots	

Method

- Wash rice, drain and place in a rice cooker.

- Heat ghee in a wok and fry shallots, garlic, ginger and spices until fragrant. Add water, screwpine leaves, evaporated milk and salt. Stir well and bring to the boil.

- Pour contents of wok into rice cooker. Cook until rice is done. Serve hot, sprinkled with raisins and shallot crisps.

VEGETABLES

Four-Colour Vegetables

Preparation time: 20 minutes   Cooking time: 20 minutes   Serves 6

Ingredients

Dried Chinese mushrooms	6, soaked to soften and halved
Salt	a pinch
Ground white pepper	a dash
Sugar	$1/4$ tsp
Sesame oil	$1/2$ tsp
Black moss (*fatt choy*)	10 g, soaked for at least 20 minutes to soften
Cooking oil	75 ml
Shanghai white cabbage (*siew pak choy*)	8 small bunches, kept whole and soaked
Ginger	2 slices, peeled and minced
Garlic	2 cloves, peeled and minced
Dried scallop	1 piece, soaked and shredded
Fried gluten balls	120 g, about 15 pieces, soaked
Carrots	10–12 slices, parboiled
Cornflour (cornstarch)	1 tsp, mixed with 1 Tbsp water

Sauce

Chicken stock	250 ml (page 175)
Sugar	$1/2$ tsp
Salt	$1/2$ tsp
Ground white pepper	$1/4$ tsp
Sesame oil	$1/2$ tsp
Chinese rice wine	1 tsp
Light soy sauce	1 tsp
Oyster sauce	1 tsp

Method

- Marinate dried Chinese mushrooms with salt, pepper, sugar and sesame oil for 30 minutes.

- Drain black moss and put to boil in a small saucepan of water with 1 Tbsp cooking oil and $1/4$ tsp salt. Cook for 1–2 minutes. Drain and leave aside.

- Rinse Shanghai white cabbage under running water to remove fine sand particles wedged between the stems. Drain and blanch in boiling water with 1 Tbsp cooking oil for 1 minute. Drain and immerse in cold water to stop vegetable from cooking further and to retain its crisp green colour. Drain and arrange vegetable on dish as preferred.

- Heat remaining cooking oil in a wok until hot and lightly brown ginger and garlic. Add Chinese mushrooms and scallop and stir-fry until fragrant.

- Add fried gluten balls and toss for 1 minute. Add black moss and carrots. Mix well.

- Pour in combined sauce ingredients and when it begins to boil, thicken with cornflour mixture. Pour over cabbage in the serving dish and serve hot.

Fried Yam Ring with Mixed Vegetables

Preparation time: 10 minutes   Cooking time: 35–40 minutes   Serves 6

Ingredients

Yam	1 kg, peeled and cut into cubes to get about 760 g cleaned weight
Salt	$1^1/_2$ tsp
Five-spice powder	1 tsp
Sugar	4 tsp
Cooking oil	1 Tbsp
Wheat starch (*tang meen fun*)	60 g
Cooking oil for deep-frying	
Lettuce	1 small head, finely sliced

Filling

Diced Chicken with Cashew Nuts	1 portion (page 18)

Method

- Place yam cubes in a steamer and steam for 25–30 minutes until soft. Mash yam cubes while still hot until free from lumps. Add salt, five-spice powder, sugar and oil. When well combined, add wheat starch flour and knead well.

- Divide yam dough into two equal portions. Lightly flour hands with wheat starch and form yam dough into two 15-cm diameter hollow rings.

- Place yam rings on a flat colander to lower into oil for deep-frying.

- Heat oil for deep-frying in a wok until hot. Lower heat to medium and deep-fry yam rings, one at a time, for about 4 minutes until golden in colour.

- Remove and place on a dish garnished with finely sliced lettuce leaves. Fill yam rings with diced chicken with cashew nuts and serve immediately.

Note:

For the best results, choose a powdery yam when making this dish.

Bean Sprouts with Salted Fish

Preparation time: 10 minutes   Cooking time: 5 minutes   Serves 4–5

Ingredients

Cooking oil	100 ml
Salted fish (threadfin)	45 g, preferably washed and finely sliced
Garlic	3 cloves, peeled and minced
Light soy sauce	$^1/_2$ Tbsp
Sesame oil	$^1/_2$ Tbsp
Bean sprouts	300 g, washed and drained
Red chilli	1, seeded and cut into strips
Spring onion (scallion)	1, split and cut into 5-cm lengths
Coriander (cilantro) leaves	1 sprig

Method

• Heat half the oil in a wok until hot. Add salted fish and fry over low heat until crisp and light golden brown. Drain and leave aside. Discard oil.

• Heat remaining oil in the same wok and lightly brown garlic. Remove and place on a serving dish. Mix with light soy sauce and sesame oil.

• Bring half a saucepan of water to a rapid boil. Add bean sprouts and scald for a few seconds.

• Drain well and place in dish of prepared sauce. Mix to combine ingredients, then sprinkle with fried salted fish. Garnish with red chilli, spring onion and coriander. Serve hot.

Stuffed Chillies (Solok Lada)

Preparation time: 20 minutes   Cooking time: 15 minutes   Serves 8

Ingredients

Spanish mackerel (*ikan tenggiri*) meat	180 g
Grated skinned coconut	150 g
Shallots	3, peeled
Sugar	1 tsp
Salt	1 tsp
Large red chillies	16, slit, seeded and soaked for 15 minutes
Coconut milk	190 ml, from $^3/_4$ grated coconut and sufficient water, mixed with a pinch of salt

Method

- Cut fish meat into large cubes and blend (process) with grated coconut and shallots until fine. Stir in sugar and salt and mix well.

- Stuff each chilli with 1 Tbsp fish mixture. Place chillies, slit side up, in a pot.

- Carefully pour in coconut milk. Cover pot and simmer gently for 15 minutes until cooked and almost dry. Dish out and serve hot.

Fried Cabbage (Kobis Masak Putih)

Preparation time: 10 minutes   Cooking time: 15 minutes   Serves 6

Ingredients

Coconut milk	1 litre, from $^{1}/_{2}$ grated coconut squeezed first for coconut cream, then add sufficient water to extract coconut milk
Red chillies	5, cut into strips
Shallots	6, peeled and sliced
Garlic	1 clove, peeled and sliced
Cabbage	300 g, cut into 1.25-cm pieces
Small prawns (shrimps)	300 g, peeled and cleaned
Coconut cream	125 ml, from $^{1}/_{2}$ grated coconut and sufficient water
Salt	$^{1}/_{2}$ tsp
Spring onion (scallion)	1, chopped

Method

- Put coconut milk, red chillies, shallots and garlic in a wok and bring to a slow boil. Simmer for 5 minutes then add cabbage.

- When cabbage is soft, add prawns, coconut cream and salt. Sprinkle in spring onion last. Remove from heat as soon as mixture comes to a boil. Serve hot.

Stuffed Bean Curd Puffs with Mixed Vegetables

Preparation time: 30 minutes   Cooking time: 20 minutes   Serves 5

Ingredients

Fried bean curd puffs (square) (*taufu pok*)	5 pieces
Cooking oil for deep-frying	
Filling*	1 portion
Cucumber	1, sliced
Tomatoes	2, sliced
Sweet soy sauce chilli dip**	1 portion

Method

• Bring a saucepan of water to the boil and scald bean curd puffs for a few seconds to remove excess oil. Drain thoroughly.

• Heat oil and deep-fry bean curd puffs until crisp. Drain on kitchen paper.

• When cool, slice each bean curd puff diagonally to obtain two triangles. Slit each piece without cutting through and stuff with the filling.

• Arrange on a serving dish garnished with cucumber and tomato slices. Serve with sweet soy sauce chilli dip.

*Filling

Ingredients

Cooking oil	1 Tbsp
Garlic	3 cloves, peeled and minced
Shallots	2, peeled and finely sliced
Shiitake mushrooms	3, about 60 g, diced
Long beans	50 g, diced
Carrots	75 g, peeled, diced small and parboiled
Bean sprouts	100 g
Cornflour (cornstarch)	1 tsp, mixed with 2 Tbsp water
Spring onion (scallion)	$^1/_2$, chopped
Coriander (cilantro) leaves	$^1/_2$ sprig, chopped

Seasoning

Salt	$^1/_2$ tsp
Sugar	1 tsp
Light soy sauce	1 tsp
Oyster sauce	1 tsp
Ground white pepper	$^1/_4$ tsp

Method

• Heat oil in a wok and lightly brown garlic and shallots. Add mushrooms and stir-fry for 1 minute. Add long beans and cook for 30 seconds. Add carrots and lastly bean sprouts. Combine seasoning ingredients and add to wok. Toss well.

• Thicken with cornflour mixture. Remove from heat and stir. Add chopped spring onion and coriander. Dish out and use as required.

**Sweet Soy Sauce Chilli Dip

Ingredients

Red chillies	3, large
Indonesian sweet soy sauce	
(*kicap manis*)	1 Tbsp
Lemon or lime juice	1 tsp
Salt	a pinch

Method

- Combine ingredients and blend in a mini food processor or blender until fine. Serve with stuffed bean curd puffs.

Pressed Bean Curd, Dried Radish and Peanuts (Chao Lup Lup)

Preparation time: 15 minutes   Cooking time: 15 minutes   Serves 4

Ingredients

Cooking oil	1 Tbsp
Onion	1, medium, peeled, halved and sliced
Garlic	2 cloves, peeled and minced
Dried salted radish (*choy poh*)	75 g, soaked for 10 minutes and chopped
Long beans	100 g, cut into 1-cm lengths
Carrot	75 g, peeled, diced and parboiled
Five spice-flavoured compressed bean curd (*ng heong taufu*)	100 g, diced
Chicken stock	2 Tbsp (page 175)
Light soy sauce	2 tsp
Sugar	1 tsp
Ground white pepper	$1/4$ tsp
Red chilli	1, seeded and cut into 1-cm pieces
Peanuts	60 g, roasted
Sesame seeds	$1/2$ Tbsp, roasted

Method

* Heat oil in a wok and lightly brown onion and garlic. Add dried salted radish and stir-fry for 1 minute. Add long beans and continue to cook for 3 minutes. Add carrot and compressed bean curd.

* Stir in chicken stock, soy sauce, sugar, pepper and red chilli. Mix well and cook until mixture is almost dry.

* Add peanuts and sesame seeds and toss well. Dish out and serve hot with rice.

Vegetable Salad (Pecal)

Preparation time: 30 minutes   Cooking time: 20 minutes   Serves 5–6

Ingredients

Water convolvulus (*kangkung*) shoots	300 g, cut into 5–cm lengths
Tender tapioca leaves	300 g, cut into 5-cm lengths
Bean sprouts	150 g
Turnip	150 g, coarsely shredded
Long beans	150 g, cut into 5-cm lengths
Carrot	1, medium, coarsely shredded
Cucumber	1, cored and coarsely shredded
Firm bean curd (*tau korn*)	2, diced and fried
Hardboiled eggs	4, peeled and quartered
Cooking oil	2 Tbsp
Tamarind pulp	2 Tbsp
Water	310 ml
Dried chillies	15, soaked to soften
Dried shrimp paste (*belachan*)	2.5-cm piece, toasted
Brown sugar	4 Tbsp
Black shrimp paste (*haeko*)	2 Tbsp
Salt	$1/2$ tsp
Peanuts	300 g, roasted and coarsely ground
Shallots	10, peeled, sliced and crisp-fried
Garlic	3 cloves, peeled, sliced and crisp-fried

Method

- Scald vegetables except cucumber separately in boiling water. Do not overcook. Drain well and arrange on a dish together with cucumber, fried bean curd and hardboiled eggs.

- Heat 1 Tbsp oil and fry tamarind paste for 1 minute over low heat. Dish out, add 125 ml water and mix well. Strain liquid.

- Heat remaining oil and fry ground chillies and dried shrimp paste over low heat until fragrant. Add strained tamarind liquid and remaining water. Bring to the boil.

- Stir in brown sugar, black shrimp paste and salt. Remove from heat and stir in ground peanuts.

- Serve vegetables with sauce separately or pour sauce over vegetables and mix well before serving. Garnish shallot and garlic crisps.

Acar Limau

Preparation time: 20 minutes   Cooking time: 25 minutes   Serves 6–8

Ingredients

Cooking oil	8 Tbsp
Dried chillies	100 g, soaked to soften and ground
Vinegar	180 ml
Water	750 ml
Sugar	6 Tbsp
Salt	2 Tbsp
Pickled limes*	100 g
Shallots	150 g, peeled
Garlic	100 g, peeled
Ginger	7.5-cm knob, shredded
Dried salted radish (*choy poh*)	100 g, cut into 1.25-cm cubes
Bilimbi (*belimbing asam*)	60 g
Prunes	100 g
Red dates (*hung cho*)	100 g
Red chillies	4, split lengthwise without cutting through
Green chillies	4, split lengthwise without cutting through
Mustard seeds	2 Tbsp, roasted
Sesame seeds	2 Tbsp, roasted

Paste

Shallots	5, peeled
Garlic	4 cloves
Cloves	7
Star anise	2 petals
Cinnamon stick	5-cm length

Method

- Combine paste ingredients and blend (process). Heat oil in a wok and fry ground ingredients until fragrant. Add ground dried chillies and fry until oil separates.

- Add vinegar, water, sugar and salt and bring to a slow boil. Simmer over low heat for 10 minutes until slightly thickened.

- Add pickled limes, shallots, garlic, shredded ginger, dried salted radish, bilimbi, prunes, red dates and chillies.

- Mix well and simmer over low heat for another 10 minutes. Add mustard seeds and sesame seeds just before removing from heat. Cool and store in an airtight container. Serve as a side dish.

*Pickled Limes

Ingredients

Vinegar	375 ml
Sugar	240 g
Salt	2 Tbsp
Limes	100 g

Method

- Boil vinegar with sugar and salt. Take off heat and add limes. Leave to cool before storing in an airtight jar. Keep for at least 2 weeks before using.

Coconut Sambal

Preparation time: 10 minutes   Cooking time: 10 minutes   Serves 8

Ingredients

Young grated skinned coconut	180 g
Dhal	1 tsp, roasted
Green chillies	3, sliced
Ginger	2 slices
Yoghurt	2 Tbsp
Salt	$1\frac{1}{4}$ tsp
Water	430 ml
Cooking oil	2 Tbsp
Mustard seeds	$\frac{1}{2}$ tsp
Curry leaves	1 sprig
Dried chillies	2, soaked to soften and cut into 0.5-cm pieces

Method

- Combine grated coconut, dhal, green chillies, ginger, yoghurt, salt and water and blend (process) into a smooth paste.

- Heat oil in saucepan and stir-fry mustard leaves, curry leaves and dried chillies.

- Pour paste in and simmer for 5 minutes. Remove from heat and use as a dip or serve with rice or thosai.

SNACKS & DESSERTS

Pak Tong Koh

Preparation time: 30 minutes   Cooking time: 50 minutes   Serves 8

Ingredients

Rice flour	300 g, sifted
Water	750 ml
Sugar	330 g
Dry or easy-blend yeast	$^1/_2$ Tbsp
Warm water	125 ml

Method

• Grease a 22-cm round cake tin with corn oil and set aside.

• Put sifted rice flour into a mixing bowl with 250 ml water and knead into a soft dough. Take 50 g of dough and place in a small saucepan with 125 ml water.

• Stir with a wooden spoon until paste dissolves, then cook over low heat, stirring constantly until a thick sticky paste forms. Let it cool, then add to remaining uncooked dough. Mix well.

• Stir 30 g sugar and yeast into warm water and add to flour mixture. Cover and leave to proof for $1^1/_2$ hours until foamy.

• Meanwhile, put remaining water and sugar in a saucepan and cook over low heat until sugar dissolves and liquid boils. Let syrup cool, then mix with rice flour mixture. Blend well and let stand for 12 minutes.

• Pour mixture into prepared cake tin. Steam covered over rapidly boiling water for 20 minutes or until cake is well-risen and firm. Cool and cut into diamond-shaped pieces to serve.

Note:

To prevent water vapour from dripping onto the cake, wipe steamer cover and wrap with a large tea towel before steaming. Ensure that the ends of the towel are not hanging down over the flames as it may catch fire.

Egg Tarts (Tarn Tart)

Preparation time: 1 hour   Baking time: 35 minutes   Makes 24

Ingredients

Dough A

Plain (all-purpose) flour	300 g
Butter	70 g, melted and cooled
Salt	$^1/_4$ tsp
Water	190 ml

Dough B

Plain (all-purpose) flour	180 g
Butter	70 g, melted and cooled
Sugar	240 g
Hot water	310 ml
Milk powder	2 Tbsp
Salt	$^1/_4$ tsp
Vanilla essence (extract)	$^1/_2$ tsp
Eggs	6, medium-sized

Method

- Sift flour for Dough A into a mixing bowl. Make a well in the centre and add butter, salt and water. Mix and knead to form a soft smooth dough. Cover dough with a tea towel and leave to rest for 30 minutes.

- Mix flour and butter for Dough B to form a soft dough. Divide into 24 equal portions. Set aside.

- Dissolve sugar in hot water and stir in milk powder and salt. Cool and add vanilla essence.

- Break eggs into a separate bowl and lightly stir with a fork. Do not beat. Pour cooled milk mixture into eggs and mix well. Strain mixture into a jug with a beak for easy pouring. Set aside.

- Take rested Dough A and roll into a long sausage-like roll. Divide into 24 equal portions. Flatten and place a round of Dough B in the centre of each portion. Enclose Dough B within Dough A and shape into a ball.

- Roll out each ball of pastry on a lightly floured surface. Fold into three layers by drawing the two opposite edges to overlap in the centre. Fold the remaining two edges to overlap in the centre as well.

- Roll out each piece into a circle about 9–10-cm wide, or roll out into a thin sheet large enough to stamp out a 9–10-cm circle with a pastry cutter. Line egg tart patty tins with pastry circles. If desired, pleat the edges decoratively.

- Pour custard mixture into pastry-lined moulds. Bake in a preheated oven at 175°C for 5 minutes, then cover tarts with aluminium foil and continue baking for a further 30–35 minutes until set. Allow to cool before serving.

Chinese Ladle Cake

Preparation time: 15 minutes   Cooking time: 15 minutes   Makes 16

Ingredients

Prawns (shrimps)	16, medium-sized, washed
Self-raising flour	180 g
Rice flour	60 g
Plain (all-purpose) flour	60 g
Salt	$1^1/_4$ tsp
Ground white pepper	$^1/_2$ tsp
Water	310 ml
Spring onion (scallion)	1, chopped
Green chillies	3, finely sliced
Onion	1, peeled and finely sliced
Cooking oil for deep-frying	

Method

- Leave prawns with shell intact or shell, but leave heads and tails intact. Trim eye section using a pair of scissors.

- Sift flours into a mixing bowl then add salt and pepper and mix into a soft batter with water. Stir in spring onion, green chillies and onion.

- Heat oil for deep-frying. Heat a ladle in hot oil for 1 minute. Remove hot ladle and pour in $1^1/_2$ Tbsp batter mixture to fill ladle. Place a prawn in the centre and press down lightly.

- Deep-fry until cake turns light golden. Loosen cake from ladle with a small knife. Let it cook further for a minute or two until cake turns golden brown. Continue until batter is used up.

- Drain on absorbent paper. Serve with chilli sauce.

Papaya Jelly Bowl

Preparation time: 10 minutes   Cooking time: 30 minutes   Serves 6–8

Ingredients

Ripe papaya	740 g, skinned and seeded
Lemon rind	grated from 1 lemon
Lemon juice	2 tsp
Agar-agar strips or powder	1 packet (strips = 25 g; powder = 13 g)
Water	1 litre
Sugar	300 g
Orange jelly crystals	1 packet, 110 g
Hot water	125 ml

Method

- Blend (process) 500 g papaya in a blender to get approximately 575 ml papaya pulp. Pour pulp into a pot and stir in lemon rind and juice. Bring to a slow boil over low heat. Allow to cool.

- If using *agar-agar* strips, wash strips first. Boil *agar-agar* strips or powder with water and sugar, stirring constantly. When *agar-agar* and sugar dissolve, remove from heat.

- Dissolve orange jelly crystals in hot water and stir into *agar-agar* mixture. Add papaya pulp and stir until well mixed. Pour mixture into a 21-cm jelly mould. Allow to cool slightly.

- Cut remaining papaya into cubes and add into cooled mixture. Leave to set in the refrigerator. Remove from mould, slice and serve cold.

Peanut Cookies (Fah Sang Peang)

Preparation time: 45 minutes   Cooking time: 20–25 minutes   Makes 100

Ingredients

Roasted peanuts	350 g
Castor (superfine) sugar	270 g
Vanilla essence (extract)	1 tsp
Plain (all-purpose) flour	350 g, sifted
Peanut oil	250 ml
Glacé cherries	as desired, cut into 0.25-cm pieces, for decoration

Egg Glaze

Egg yolks	2, lightly beaten
Milk	2 tsp

Method

- Blend (process) peanuts in an electric blender until fine and crumbly.

- In a large mixing bowl, combine ground peanuts, sugar, vanilla essence and flour. Make a well in the centre and pour in peanut oil. Mix well with a wooden spoon.

- Lightly run through the mixture with fingers to bind it into a crumbly dough.

- Make egg glaze by combining egg yolks with milk.

- Shape dough into balls about the size of a cherry. Make a shallow depression in each ball with the pointed end of a chopstick. Press a piece of glacé cherry into each depression and brush cookies well with egg glaze.

- Bake in a preheated oven at 175°C for 20–25 minutes or until golden brown. Remove cookies gently to avoid breaking them. Cool completely before serving or storing in an airtight jar.

Kuih Nagasari

Preparation time: 30 minutes   Cooking time: 30 minutes   Makes 16

Ingredients

Rice flour	240 g
Water	500 ml
Coconut milk	875 ml, from 1 grated coconut and sufficient water
Screwpine (pandan) leaves	2, knotted
Salt	$1/2$ tsp
Banana leaves	16, cut into 18 x 15-cm pieces, scalded
Small ripe bananas (*pisang raja*)	8, peeled and halved lengthwise

Method

- Sift rice flour into a bowl, add water and blend mixture until smooth.

- Place coconut milk, screwpine leaves and salt in a saucepan and bring to a slow boil. Add rice flour batter and stir with a wooden spoon for approximately 5 minutes until mixture turns into a smooth paste. Remove from heat.

- Place a spoonful of cooked mixture in the centre of each banana leaf. Fold one side of banana leaf over to flatten mixture into a small rectangle. Lift folded flap of banana leaf and top flattened mixture with a piece of banana. Cover with another spoonful of cooked mixture. Fold banana leaf to overlap lengthwise to cover mixture. Tuck the other ends under to make a neat parcel. Continue until all 16 parcels are ready.

- Steam for 20 minutes and serve hot or cold.

Kuih Koleh-koleh Kacang

Preparation time: 15 minutes   Cooking time: 1 hour 10 minutes   Serves 10–12

Ingredients

Topping
Coconut cream	250 ml, from 1 grated coconut and sufficient water

Kuih
Green (mung) beans	300 g, soaked for at least 2 hours or overnight
Coconut milk	750 ml, from $1^1/_2$ grated coconuts and sufficient water
Palm sugar (*gula Melaka*)	450 g, cut into small pieces
Water	125 ml
Screwpine (pandan) leaves	2, shredded and knotted

Method

- Prepare topping. Put coconut cream into a wok and stir over low heat with a wooden spatula for 30–35 minutes. Oil will separate from coconut residue. Continue stirring until coconut residue turns a rich brown colour. Remove from heat and drain. Set aside.

- Prepare kuih. Wash green beans and place into a pressure cooker with 1 litre water. Pressure cook for 20 minutes.

- Put cooked beans in a blender (processor) with coconut milk and blend until fine. Set aside. For finer blending, do this three times. If mixture is still thick and blender is not turning well, add a little extra coconut milk.

- Combine palm sugar with water in a heatproof (flameproof) bowl and stir constantly over heat to melt sugar. Strain into blended bean mixture. Mix well.

- Pour mixture into a wok, add screwpine leaves and stir continuously with a wooden spatula over low heat for 15 minutes or until it becomes a thick paste. Do not allow mixture to stick to bottom of wok. To test if paste is thick enough, make a figure 8 with the spatula. If it holds well, the paste is of the right consistency. Discard screwpine leaves.

- Spoon mixture into an 18 x 27-cm shallow tin and smooth the surface while hot with a piece of banana leaf or a butter knife. Top with prepared coconut residue crisps. Leave to cool thoroughly before cutting to serve.

Note:

Green pea flour (hoon kway powder), if available, can be used instead of green beans. Simply sift the same amount of flour and stir in coconut milk without adding water.

Kuih Wajik

Preparation time: 20 minutes   Cooking time: 1 hour   Makes 28 pieces

Ingredients

Water	125 ml
Palm sugar (*gula Melaka*)	300 g, cut into small pieces
Granulated sugar	60 g
Screwpine (pandan) leaves	8, 3 knotted and 5 reserved
Glutinous rice	600 g, soaked overnight
Coconut cream	500 ml, from 2 grated coconuts and sufficient water, mixed with a pinch of salt

Method

• Combine water, palm sugar, granulated sugar and knotted screwpine leaves in a saucepan and stir over low heat until sugar dissolves. Discard screwpine leaves and strain syrup.

• Line the base of a steaming tray with a piece of muslin and place a few extra blades of screwpine leaves on the cloth.

• Spread glutinous rice over screwpine leaves and steam for 45 minutes.

• Transfer steamed rice into a pan and mix with coconut milk and strained syrup. Cook mixture over low heat, stirring continuously until mixture becomes thick and a rich oily brown.

• Spread mixture onto an 18 x 28-cm tray and allow to cool and harden. Cut to serve.

Kuih Bingka Telur

Preparation time: 20 minutes   Cooking time: 1 hour   Makes 25

Ingredients

Eggs	6, lightly beaten
Granulated sugar	270 g
Plain (all-purpose) flour	195 g, sifted
Butter	30 g, melted
Salt	a pinch
Vanilla essence (extract)	1 tsp
Coconut milk	1 litre, from 3 grated coconuts and sufficient water
Yellow food colouring	2–3 drops

Method

- Line the base of a 22-cm square cake tin with greased greaseproof paper.

- Lightly stir eggs and sugar together. Add sifted flour gradually to egg mixture and mix well.

- Stir in melted butter, salt, vanilla essence and coconut milk a little at a time until fully combined.

- Add yellow colouring and strain mixture into prepared tin.

- Bake in a preheated oven at 175°C for 45 minutes, then lower temperature to 150°C and bake a further 15 minutes until set.

- Leave to cool in the tin before cutting to serve.

Gulab Jamun

Preparation time: 15 minutes   Cooking time: 20 minutes   Makes 20

Ingredients

Self-raising flour	75 g
Full-cream milk powder	300 g
Ghee (clarified butter)	30 g
Evaporated milk	90 ml
Ghee or corn oil for frying	

Syrup

Sugar	560 g
Water	1 litre

Method

• Prepare syrup. In a saucepan, combine sugar and water and bring to the boil until sugar is dissolved. Leave to cool.

• Sift self-raising flour and milk powder into a large bowl. Rub in ghee, then add enough evaporated milk to give a firm but pliable dough. Form into small balls.

• Heat ghee or corn oil for deep-frying in a wok and deep-fry over low heat until *gulab jamun* are dark golden in colour.

• Remove *gulab jamun* and place them in prepared syrup in a covered container. Allow to cool completely and serve at room temperature or chilled.

Pie Tee

Preparation time: 1 hour   Cooking time: 1 hour 30 minutes   Makes 38

Ingredients

Pie Tee Shells

Plain (all-purpose) flour	90 g
Rice flour	1 Tbsp
Salt	$^1/_4$ tsp
Egg	1, beaten
Water	190 ml
Cooking oil for deep-frying	
Lettuce	$^1/_2$ a head, torn into small pieces
Crisp-fried shallots	
Coriander (cilantro) leaves	

Filling

Cooking oil	3 Tbsp
Garlic	4 cloves, peeled and minced
Turnip (*bangkwang*)	450 g, peeled, finely shredded and squeezed to get rid of excess water
Chicken or pork	240 g, diced
Prawns (shrimps)	240 g, peeled, cleaned and diced
Crabmeat	90 g

Seasoning

Five-spice powder	$^1/_4$ tsp
Salt	1 tsp
Ground white pepper	$^1/_4$ tsp

Method

- Prepare pie tee shells. Sift plain and rice flours into a small bowl. Add salt. Stir in egg and mix with water to make a smooth runny batter. Strain if batter is lumpy.

- Heat oil for deep-frying in a deep pan and heat pie tee mould in hot oil for a minute. Remove hot mould and dip in batter. Place mould in hot oil until pie tee is golden in colour. Loosen pie tee from mould by shaking it gently or using a fork to push it down to drain on absorbent paper. Continue until batter is used up. Leave shells to cool and store in an airtight container until required.

- Prepare filling. Heat oil in a wok and lightly brown minced garlic. Add turnip and stir-fry, then add chicken or pork and prawns.

- Stir in seasoning ingredients and crabmeat. Simmer until quite dry, then dish up and leave to cool.

- To serve, line pie tee shell with a small piece of lettuce. Spoon in 2 tsp filling and garnish with crispy shallots and coriander leaves. Serve with chilli sauce if preferred. Serve immediately to avoid pie tee shells from becoming soggy.

Sung Koh

Preparation time: 15 hours   Cooking time: 1 hour   Makes one 22.5-cm round cake

Ingredients

Cooked rice	50 g (cooked using more water for softer grains)
Castor (superfine) sugar	1 tsp
Ragi (*chow peang*)	1/2 piece, about 8 g, pounded
Water	355 ml
Rice flour	250 g, sifted
Plain (all-purpose) flour	50 g, sifted
Yellow food colouring	a few drops
Castor (superfine) sugar	150 g
Fruit salt	1 Tbsp

Method

- Combine cooked rice, castor sugar, *ragi* and 30 ml water. Mix well and leave in an airtight plastic container for 12 hours to ferment.

- Place fermented mixture into a blender (processor). Pour in half the remaining amount of water and blend until well combined.

- Pour mixture out into a bowl and mix in rice flour and plain flour. Stir in remaining water and strain into a clean mixing bowl. Cover with a damp tea towel and set aside for 3 hours.

- Stir in yellow food colouring, castor sugar and fruit salt and mix until well combined using a balloon whisk. Mix until sugar completely dissolves.

- Turn mixture out into a greased 22.5-cm round baking tin. Steam over medium heat for 20 minutes then increase heat and steam for a further 40 minutes. Slice and serve warm or cool.

Note:

Ragi *is a type of yeast. It is also known as* jiu piah *in Hokkien.* Ragi *is available from some wet market stalls and Chinese herbal medicine shops.*

Nyonya Kuih Mah Chee

Preparation time: 30 minutes   Cooking time: 20 minutes   Makes 15

Ingredients

Peanuts	60 g, roasted and coarsely ground
Grated skinned coconut	120 g
Brown sugar	75 g
Salt	$1/4$ tsp
Glutinous rice flour	360 g
Water	250 ml
Green (mung) bean flour	2 Tbsp, dry-roasted

Method

- Put peanuts, grated coconut, brown sugar and salt in a wok and stir-fry over low heat for 10 minutes. Remove and set aside to cool.

- Sift glutinous rice flour into a mixing bowl and add enough water to form a soft dough. Divide into 15 portions and roll into balls.

- Flatten each ball of dough slightly and fill with 1 tsp of filling. Pinch edges to seal filling. Roll and lightly flatten.

- Bring a pot of water to the boil. Drop in rice balls. Remove with a slotted spoon as soon as they float to the surface. Allow to dry a little before coating with roasted green bean flour.

Note:

Green (mung) bean flour is also known as luk tow fun *in Cantonese. It is available from Chinese provision stores.*

Kek Masam Manis

Preparation time: 20 minutes   Cooking time: 42 minutes   Makes one 21-cm round cake

Ingredients

Eggs	5, yolks and whites separated
Castor (superfine) sugar	150 g
Butter	250 g
Condensed milk	198 g ($^1/_2$ can)
Vanilla essence (extract)	1 tsp
Cream (soda) crackers	150 g, pounded and sifted
Green food colouring	$^1/_4$ tsp
Haw flakes (round)	15 packs

Method

- Whisk egg whites until stiff, then gradually add sugar a spoonful at a time, beating well after each addition.

- In a separate bowl, cream butter, condensed milk and vanilla essence until light and fluffy. Add egg yolks one at a time, beating well after each addition.

- Add egg yolk mixture to egg white mixture. Combine lightly and evenly. Fold in pounded crackers and divide mixture into two equal portions. Colour one portion green.

- Line the base of a 21-cm round cake tin with greased greaseproof paper. Spread a third of green mixture evenly onto base of lined tin. Arrange three packets of haw flakes on surface.

- Steam over rapid boiling water for 7 minutes. Remove from steamer and spread a third of yellow mixture over steamed layer. Arrange another three packets of haw flakes on top and return to steamer for 7 minutes. Repeat procedure, alternating layers with remaining green and yellow mixtures and haw flakes.

- Allow cake to cool in the tin for 15 minutes before turning out onto a wire rack to cool thoroughly. When cool, slice to serve.

Sago Pudding

Preparation time: 30 minutes   Cooking time: 30 minutes   Serves 8

Ingredients

Pearl sago	240 g
Egg white	1
Salt	a pinch
Palm sugar (*gula Melaka*) syrup	1 portion (page 175)
Coconut milk	800 ml from $1^1/_2$ grated coconuts and sufficient water, mixed with a pinch of salt

Method

- Wash sago and drain. Place in a saucepan of boiling water, stir well and cook for about 10 minutes until sago becomes transparent. Pour into a large sieve and place under running water. Stir to wash away excess starch. Stand sieve over a bowl to allow water to drain off completely.

- Whisk egg white and salt until stiff, then fold into sago. Spoon mixture into small jelly moulds and chill in the refrigerator while preparing palm syrup and coconut milk.

- Remove chilled sago from refrigerator and pop out of moulds. Place on individual serving dishes and top sago pudding with coconut milk and palm syrup to taste.

Banana Coconut Cream with Palm Syrup

Preparation time: 10 minutes   Cooking time: 15 minutes   Makes 15

Ingredients

Green pea flour (*hoon kway* powder)	1 packet, 85 g
Coconut milk	750 ml, from 1 grated coconut and sufficient water
Vanilla essence	$^1/_2$ tsp
Banana essence	$^1/_4$ tsp
Sugar	90 g
Evaporated milk	3 Tbsp
Bananas	3, peeled and sliced
Palm sugar (*gula Melaka*) syrup	1 portion (page 175)

Method

- Blend green pea flour with a little coconut milk until smooth. Add remaining coconut milk, vanilla essence, banana essence and sugar. Cook over low heat, stirring constantly with a wooden spoon.

- When mixture is hot, stir in evaporated milk and continue stirring until mixture boils and thickens. Remove from heat and stir in banana slices.

- Pour mixture into a 17 x 27-cm tray. Allow to cool then chill in the refrigerator.

- When cold, stamp out rounds with a pastry cutter or cut into squares. Serve in individual serving dishes topped with a little palm sugar syrup.

Puteri Berendam

Preparation time: 15 minutes   Cooking time: 20 minutes   Serves 4–6

Ingredients

Filling

Palm sugar (*gula Melaka*)	60 g, chopped
Water	4 Tbsp
Salt	a pinch
Grated skinned coconut	120 g

Dough

Glutinous rice flour	150 g, sifted
Water	250 ml
Green food colouring	a few drops

Coconut milk

Coconut cream	375 ml, from 1 grated coconut and sufficient water
Sugar	3 Tbsp
Salt	$1/4$ tsp
Flour	$1/2$ Tbsp
Screwpine (pandan) leaves	3, knotted

Method

- Make filling. Combine palm sugar, water and salt in a small saucepan and stir over low heat until sugar dissolves. Strain syrup into a wok and add grated coconut. Fry until coconut is evenly coated with syrup. Dish out and cool.

- Make dough. Knead rice flour, water and colouring into a firm dough. Form into small marble-sized balls. Flatten each ball lightly and fill with a teaspoonful of filling. Press edges together and shape into balls.

- Boil half a pan of water and add glutinous rice balls a few at a time. As soon as they float to the surface, remove with a perforated ladle.

- Prepare coconut milk. Mix coconut cream, sugar, salt and flour in a pan until smooth. Add screwpine leaves and bring to the boil, stirring continuously. Add glutinous rice balls and simmer for a few minutes until coconut milk thickens. Serve hot in individual bowls.

Kuih Pelita/Tepung Pelita

Preparation time: 50 minutes   Cooking time: 15 minutes   Makes 34

Ingredients

Banana leaves	10–12, cut into 5 x 10-cm sheets
Granulated sugar	

Coconut Topping

Rice flour	60 g, sifted
Sugar	30 g
Coconut cream	810 ml, from 3 grated coconuts and sufficient water
Salt	$^3/_4$ tsp

Rice Flour Layer

Rice flour	225 g, sifted
Sugar	60 g
Screwpine (pandan) leaves	8, cut into small pieces
Coconut milk	1.9 litres, from same 3 grated coconuts squeezed for coconut cream and sufficient water
Salt	$^1/_4$ tsp
Vanilla essence	1 tsp
Green food colouring	a few drops (optional)

Method

- Scald banana leaves and dry with a tea towel. Fold into boat shapes and secure by stapling the two folded ends. Fill each boat with 1 Tbsp granulated sugar and arrange boats in neat rows, one against the other on steaming trays. This will help the boats keep their shape when filled.

- Prepare rice flour layer. Place rice flour into a large saucepan and add sugar.

- Put screwpine leaves with half the coconut milk and blend in an electric blender. Strain mixture. Gradually add mixture to rice flour with remaining coconut milk and mix well with salt, vanilla essence and green colouring, if desired. Bring mixture to a slow boil, stirring all the time with a wooden spoon until thick, glossy and smooth.

- Fill boats with 2 Tbsp cooked mixture while it is still hot. Set filled boats aside.

- Cook coconut topping. Sift remaining rice flour into a saucepan, add sugar and gradually stir in coconut cream with salt. Cook mixture over medium heat, stirring all the time until mixture is thick, glossy and smooth. Spoon 1 Tbsp hot coconut topping over green layer.

- Steam over rapidly boiling water for 15 minutes. Allow to cool thoroughly before serving.

Puttu

Preparation time: 15 minutes   Cooking time: 20 minutes   Serves 4–5

Ingredients

Rice flour	360 g, sifted + 2 tsp extra
Salt	$^1/_2$ tsp
Boiling water	250 ml
Grated coconut	60 g
Sugar	1 tsp

Method

- Combine rice flour and salt in a bowl. Add boiling water and mix with a wooden spoon, then rub gently with the fingertips to combine mixture into a stiff, crumbly dough.

- Place a piece of greaseproof paper on a work surface. Turn dough onto the paper and sprinkle grated coconut and extra rice flour over dough. Cut mixture with a pastry or biscuit cutter into pea-size crumbs. Sprinkle with sugar and mix gently with the fingertips.

- Line a steamer tray with a piece of damp muslin cloth. Place mixture on top and bring edges of muslin cloth over to cover.

- Steam over rapidly boiling water for 10 minutes. Serve puttu with grated coconut and palm sugar (*gula Melaka*), or fish, chicken or mutton curry.

Note:

Puttu *should ideally be steamed in a bamboo cylinder. This is time consuming but worth trying as it gives a special fragrance to the dish. The bamboo cylinder is filled with alternating layers of puttu mixture and grated coconut, then pressed down gently and steamed. The method given in this recipe is an improvised, time-saving one. To ensure that the puttu turns out soft, the water has to be at boiling point and added immediately to the flour. This partly helps to cook the dough.*

Tepung Bungkus

Preparation time: 40 minutes   Cooking time: 20 minutes   Makes 16

Ingredients

Rice flour	240 g
Water	500 ml
Coconut milk	750 ml, from 1 grated coconut and sufficient water
Sugar	210 g
Screwpine (pandan) leaves	2, knotted
Salt	$1/4$ tsp

Filling

Palm sugar (*gula Melaka*)	90 g, chopped
Water	125 ml
Grated young coconut	180 g
Salt	$1/4$ tsp
Banana leaves	16, cut into 18 x 15-cm pieces, scalded

Method

- Sift rice flour into a bowl, add water and blend until smooth. Set aside.

- Combine coconut milk, sugar, screwpine leaves and salt in a saucepan over low heat. Stir to dissolve sugar.

- Add rice flour batter and stir with a wooden spoon for approximately 5 minutes until mixture is cooked and turns into a smooth paste. Remove from heat.

- Make filling by combining palm sugar and water in a small saucepan over low heat. Stir until sugar dissolves. Strain.

- Place strained syrup in a wok with grated coconut and salt and fry until evenly coated. Dish out and cool. Form into marble-sized balls. Set aside.

- Place a spoonful of cooked rice flour paste in the centre of each banana leaf sheet. Fold one side of banana leaf over to flatten paste into a small rectangle.

- Place two marble-sized balls of filling in the centre about 1.25 cm apart. Place another spoonful of rice flour paste on top of coconut filling. Fold banana leaf to overlap lengthwise over mixture and tuck the other ends underneath. Repeat until paste and filling are used up.

- Steam parcels for 20 minutes. Serve hot or chilled.

Kuih Serimuka

Preparation time: 30 minutes   Cooking time: 45 minutes   Makes 24

Ingredients

Top Layer

Eggs	4
Sugar	180 g
Plain (all-purpose) flour	80 g
Tapioca flour	30 g
Coconut cream	375 ml, from 1 grated coconut and sufficient water
Screwpine (pandan) leaf juice	4 Tbsp
Green food colouring	2–3 drops
Vanilla essence	$1/2$ tsp

Bottom Layer

Glutinous rice	480 g
Coconut milk	560 ml, from $1/2$ grated coconut and 375 ml water
Salt	$1^{1}/_{4}$ tsp

Method

- Prepare top layer. Stir eggs and sugar together in a bowl. Do not beat.

- Sift in plain and tapioca flours. Mix well. Gradually pour in coconut cream, screwpine juice, green colouring and vanilla essence. Strain to remove lumps. Set aside.

- Wash glutinous rice and place into a 25–27-cm baking tin. Pour in enough coconut milk to cover the rice. Stir in salt.

- Steam glutinous rice for 20–25 minutes. When cooked, press down firmly with the back of a spoon. Pour in top layer and steam for a further 20 minutes over medium heat. Allow to cool before cutting to serve.

Glossary

Screwpine (Pandan) Leaves
These long bladed, dark green leaves are used for their special fragrance. Desserts made with coconut milk will not taste the same without these aromatic leaves.

Lesser Galangal (*Cekur*) Leaves
This miniature member of the ginger family has leaves that are about 10-cm long and rhizomes less than 2.5-cm long. It has a very pronounced aromatic flavour.

Polygonum (Laksa) Leaves (*Daun Kesum*)
These thin, narrow pointed leaves are about 4-cm long and 1-cm wide. They are commonly used to flavour laksa gravy and also eaten raw in Thai salads.

Sweet Basil (*Selasih*)
The leaves are dark green, smooth and egg-shaped with a pointed tip. They are valued for their sweet aroma and fragrance, and commonly used in Thai, Malaysian and Vietnamese cooking.

Galangal (*Lengkuas*)
A rhizome with a delicate flavour, galangal is used extensively in South East Asian cooking, especially in curries.

Tapioca Leaves
The leaves are dark green and palm-shaped with serrated edges. The old leaves are usually washed and used as a natural tenderiser for meat, while the very young leaves are used in spicy salads.

Lemongrass (*Serai*)

A tall grass that grows in clumps, lemongrass is usually sold with the leaves already trimmed. For grinding, the outer layer is usually removed before use. When a recipe calls for lightly crushed lemongrass, smash lightly with a pestle or the flat surface of a cleaver.

Spring Onion (Scallion)

A young onion with an immature bulb. The round, hollow leaves and unformed bulb have a mild flavour and are used for garnishing and flavouring.

Torch Ginger Bud (*Bunga Kantan*)

This bud of the wild ginger plant has a lovely pink colour and thick, waxy petals. It adds a lovely fragrance to dishes.

Bilimbi (Belimbing Asam)

A small, light green fruit with a sourish taste. Used in curries and sambals to give an appetising tangy flavour to the dish. It is also used to tenderise meat.

Cencaluk

These fermented baby shrimps are sold in jars or bottles and have a strong, fishy flavour. For those who have acquired a taste for it, it makes an appetising dish.

Stink Beans (*Petai*)

Indigenous to Malaysia, these strong-smelling beans are oval in shape and light green in colour. The best beans are said to be found near Bidor, Perak, where they are known as *petai* paddy. The beans have medicinal value and are used as a cure for diabetes. They are known to have a diuretic effect when taken. They can be eaten raw or cooked in *sambal tumis* and curry.

Black Shrimp Paste (*Haeko*)

This thick dark paste is sold in plastic jars. It is made from prawns (shrimps) and is usually diluted with a little warm water before use.

Polyconattum (*Yok Chok*)
Also known as Solomon's seal, this herb has a mild sweet flavour and is used in the preparation of Beggar's chicken and tea eggs.

Astragalus (*Pak Kei*)
These pale yellow roots are believed to improve poor blood circulation and fatigue.

Haw Flakes
Haw flakes are made from the haw fruit and are commonly available as thin, round flakes. They are sold in most local sweet shops as a snack. They are enjoyed for their sweet and sour flavour.

Chinese Red Dates (Hung Cho)
These sweet dried red dates are commonly used both in sweet and savoury soups. They impart a sweet flavour to dishes.

Ragi (*Chow Peang*), Sweet Variety
These Chinese yeast cakes are sold in Chinese sundry or medicinal shops. There are two varieties available — sweet and spicy. The sweet variety is a flat white disc and the spicy variety is round like a marble. They are used when making Chinese sweet cakes and fermenting glutinous rice wine.

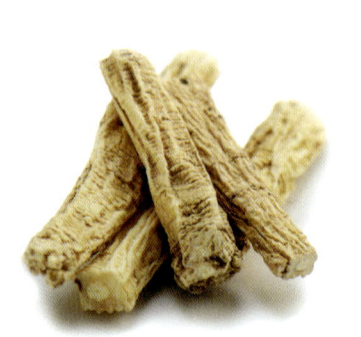

Codonopsitis (*Tong Sum*)
This root herb is brewed as a tonic to nourish the blood and improve blood circulation.

Chinese Angelica Root (*Tong Kwai*)
A medicinal root popularly taken by Chinese women after childbirth to alleviate pain and prevent haemorrhage. It has a distinctive, pungent aroma and is also commonly used in Chinese cooking.

Basic Recipes

Shallot Oil

Ingredients

Cooking oil	375 ml
Shallots	30, peeled and thinly sliced

Method

- Heat oil in a wok. Fry sliced shallots, stirring constantly over low heat until pale brown.

- Remove shallots with a perforated ladle to drain on absorbent kitchen paper. When cool, store in an airtight container. Fried shallots keep for several weeks in the refrigerator and can be used as garnish.

- Allow oil in wok to cool before storing in a clean dry container at room temperature. This shallot oil will keep indefinitely and can be used for steaming and stir-frying.

Rice Cake

Ingredients

Rice flour	300 g
Salt	$1/2$ tsp
Water	940 ml
Alkaline water	1 tsp
Borax (optional)	a pinch
Shallot oil	$1^1/2$ Tbsp

Method

- Sieve rice flour into a mixing bowl and add salt and water. Stir well until free from lumps.

- Add alkaline water, borax and shallot oil. Mix well.

- Place a greased 22-cm round cake tin in a steamer. Cover and bring water to the boil.

- When water is boiling, pour mixture into heated cake tin and cover steamer. Leave to steam over boiling water on medium heat for 1 hour.

- Remove rice cake from steamer and cool completely before cutting. Use as required.

Palm Syrup

Ingredients

Palm sugar (*gula Melaka*)	240 g, chopped
Granulated sugar	30 g
Water	250 ml
Screwpine (pandan) leaves	2, knotted

Method

- Place palm sugar, granulated sugar, water and screwpine leaves into a saucepan and boil over low heat until sugar is dissolved. Strain and discard screwpine leaves. Use as required.

Chilli Paste

Ingredients

Dried chillies	25, cut, seeded and soaked to soften

Method

- Place dried chillies in an electric blender. Add a pinch of salt and just enough water to blend (process) into a fine paste.

- Use as required. Chilli paste can be stored in the freezer for up to 3 weeks.

Chicken stock

Ingredients

Chicken carcasses	8, quartered and cleaned
Water	3–3.5 litres

Method

- Combine chicken bones and water in a large, deep saucepan. Bring to the boil, reduce heat and simmer, covered, over low heat for 1 hour.

- Strain stock using a large fine sieve. Allow to cool thoroughly.

- Refrigerate for 2–3 hours until oil rises and sets on the surface. Skim off the oil. Use as required or freeze stock in small portions. Frozen stock will keep for several weeks. Thaw and use as required.

Weights & Measures

Quantities for this book are given in Metric and American (spoon and cup) measures.
Standard spoon and cup measurements used are: 1 teaspoon = 5 ml, 1 tablespoon = 15 ml,
1 cup = 250 ml. All measures are level unless otherwise stated.

LIQUID AND VOLUME MEASURES

Metric	Imperial	American
5 ml	$1/6$ fl oz	1 teaspoon
10 ml	$1/3$ fl oz	1 dessertspoon
15 ml	$1/2$ fl oz	1 tablespoon
60 ml	2 fl oz	$1/4$ cup (4 tablespoons)
85 ml	$2^1/2$ fl oz	$1/3$ cup
90 ml	3 fl oz	$3/8$ cup (6 tablespoons)
125 ml	4 fl oz	$1/2$ cup
180 ml	6 fl oz	$3/4$ cup
250 ml	8 fl oz	1 cup
300 ml	10 fl oz ($1/2$ pint)	$1^1/4$ cups
375 ml	12 fl oz	$1^1/2$ cups
435 ml	14 fl oz	$1^3/4$ cups
500 ml	16 fl oz	2 cups
625 ml	20 fl oz (1 pint)	$2^1/2$ cups
750 ml	24 fl oz ($1^1/5$ pints)	3 cups
1 litre	32 fl oz ($1^3/5$ pints)	4 cups
1.25 litres	40 fl oz (2 pints)	5 cups
1.5 litres	48 fl oz ($2^2/5$ pints)	6 cups
2.5 litres	80 fl oz (4 pints)	10 cups

DRY MEASURES

Metric	Imperial
30 grams	1 ounce
45 grams	$1^1/2$ ounces
55 grams	2 ounces
70 grams	$2^1/2$ ounces
85 grams	3 ounces
100 grams	$3^1/2$ ounces
110 grams	4 ounces
125 grams	$4^1/2$ ounces
140 grams	5 ounces
280 grams	10 ounces
450 grams	16 ounces (1 pound)
500 grams	1 pound, $1^1/2$ ounces
700 grams	$1^1/2$ pounds
800 grams	$1^3/4$ pounds
1 kilogram	2 pounds, 3 ounces
1.5 kilograms	3 pounds, $4^1/2$ ounces
2 kilograms	4 pounds, 6 ounces

LENGTH

Metric	Imperial
0.5 cm	$1/4$ inch
1 cm	$1/2$ inch
1.5 cm	$3/4$ inch
2.5 cm	1 inch

OVEN TEMPERATURE

	°C	°F	Gas Regulo
Very slow	120	250	1
Slow	150	300	2
Moderately slow	160	325	3
Moderate	180	350	4
Moderately hot	190/200	370/400	5/6
Hot	210/220	410/440	6/7
Very hot	230	450	8
Super hot	250/290	475/550	9/10

ABBREVIATION

Tbsp	tablespoon
tsp	teaspoon
kg	kilogram
g	gram
l	litres
ml	millilitre